Laszlo Trankovits

111 Places
in Jerusalem
That You
Shouldn't Miss

T0352183

emons:

© Emons Verlag GmbH
All rights reserved
© Photographs: Laszlo Trankovits, except:
ch. 1 above: Anatoly Shenfeld, below: Sandra Kaufman; ch. 3: Mikaela Burstow;
ch. 15: Amir Balaban; ch. 22: shutterstock.com/Phish Photography;
ch. 34: Ricki Rachman; ch. 35: Ulrich Sahm; ch. 40: Igor Favorov;
ch. 41: Glen Whisky Bar; ch. 42: Gush Katuf Museum; ch. 44: Dana Decktor;
ch. 49: shutterstock.com/Alon Adika; ch. 50: Yonatan Swed; ch. 68: Oriya Tadmor;
ch. 71: Notre Dame Center; ch. 83, 93: Israel Museum, Elie Posner;
ch. 86, 87: shutterstock.com/Jose HERNANDEZ Camera 51;
ch. 88: shutterstock.com/salajean; ch. 90: shutterstock.com/mikhail;
ch. 96: Ivan Tihienko; ch. 102: Moshe Menagen
© Cover motif: shutterstock.com/Shahril KHMD
Layout: Eva Kraskes, based on a design
by Lübbeke | Naumann | Thoben
English translation: John Sykes, Cologne
Maps: altancicek.design, www.altancicek.de
Basic cartographical information from Openstreetmap,
© OpenStreetMap-Mitwirkende, ODbL
Printing and binding: Lensing Druck GmbH & Co. KG,
Feldbachacker 16, 44149 Dortmund
Printed in Germany 2019
ISBN 978-3-7408-0320-9
First edition

Did you enjoy it? Do you want more?
Join us in uncovering new places around the world on:
www.111places.com

Foreword

Jerusalem is unique, incomparable. Fought over, destroyed and rebuilt over a period of 3,000 years. No end to its dramatic story is in sight. No place in the world is more important than this relatively small city in the hills of Judaea. For billions of Christians it is the place where Jesus was crucified and resurrected; for billions of Muslims the site where Mohammed ascended into heaven. For 15 million Jews all over the world, however, Jerusalem is the heart of their history and their religion. Both Israelis and Palestinians claim Jerusalem as their capital city.

For a long time, Jerusalem was regarded as the centre of the world, as the interface between heaven and earth. It is the site of biblical prophecies and miracles, of historical intrigues and crimes. The city was the stage for kings, conquerors, prophets and saints. Legends and secrets surround the palaces, ruins, temples, churches and tombs. Ancient traditions, commandments and rites are part of everyday life here. In some quarters the laws of the Old Testament still prevail, while other districts are like a shtetl from eastern Europe. In some places, Ottoman law applies. Minorities such as Druze or Samaritans as well as obscure sects and utopians have created worlds of their own in their quarters and niches.

Yet Jerusalem is also a modern city with daring architecture and teeming markets, with dozens of ambitious theatres and 80 museums, some of them spectacular, with remarkable restaurants, pubs and bars. The city is a bastion of the arts and sciences, an international magnet for researchers, artists and writers. Jerusalem was probably never more magnificent, splendid and diverse than it is today. For unbelievable sums running into the billions, it has been built and excavated, restored and beautified. For visitors, a paradise of discoveries awaits.

111 Places

1 AManTo EART

Experimental dance and a bridge to Japan

The café and arts centre are situated in the picturesque Nahlaot quarter with its winding lanes, small squares, hidden courtyards and numerous synagogues. The project does not fit in with this orthodox neighbourhood, where a venue that holds events with experimental dance on the Shabbat amounts to sacrilege. Fortunately, the thick walls of the 150-year-old building absorb all the sounds.

The initiator of the centre is Yuko Imazaike. Here she sells fair-trade goods and natural products from Israel and the Palestinian territories, organises flea markets, and puts on dance, sushi and Arabic courses, as well as all kinds of art projects. Born in Japan in 1984, Yuko Imazaike attended ballet school and became a member of a dance ensemble with which she toured worldwide. Following performances in Israel, she was so fascinated by the country that she decided to stay.

Alongside her activities as a dancer on the stage and for television, she developed her ambitious project: art as a means of connecting all aspects of life. She wanted her centre to be a Zen Buddhist salon, a modern dance theatre, an alternative corner shop, an original place of education and a guesthouse – one of the beds is placed on the gallery above the stage. At the same time, in the 'heavenly city' she aims to give Jews, Christians and Muslims a cultural link to Japan, where people have a traditional longing for spiritual and earthly harmony. The name of the institution expresses this crossing of cultural borders. AManTo refers to the Japanese avant-garde dancer Jun Amanto. 'EART' combines the English words 'heart', 'art' and 'earth'. Imazaike promises that 'everyone who visits AManTo becomes a heavenly person'. Yet her events are earth-bound and ecological. Her vegetarian sushi courses only use foods that are not sold on the markets as they have small faults.

Address 21 Yosef Haim, Nahlaot, Jerusalem 9452424, +972 52 8839577, www.amantoeartjerusalem.com | **Getting there** Bus 7 or 19 to Bezalel/Nissim Bear; bus 25, 32, 45, 66, 74, 75 or 78 to Mahane Yehuda Market/Agripas | **Hours** Café/salon Sun–Thu noon–10pm, Fri noon–4pm, Sat 7–10pm | **Tip** The synagogue of Ades, built in 1901 by Syrian immigrants, is famous for its beauty. The interiors are adorned with precious paintings, carvings and mosaics. Visits by arrangement by telephone (1 Beersheba Street, at the corner of Shilo Street, +972 50 5548376).

2 — Aqua Bella

Ruins of a Crusader castle in an idyllic park

The ruins of a castle built by the Crusaders lie in a hilly, idyllic park with small springs, a stream, well-tended gardens and many trees – pomegranate, fig and olive trees, as well as large oaks. The beauty of this spot prompted the Crusaders who built the castle in the 12th century to call it the 'lovely waters', in Latin 'Aqua Bella'. In Arabic, its name is Deir al Benat, meaning 'Nunnery of Daughters'. However, this charming place in the En Hemed National Park, today a popular destination for trippers from Jerusalem, was used as a fortification in the possession of the Order of Knights of St John for a short time only.

In 1168, following the victorious First Crusade, the Knights of St John acquired the fortress-like building from a local Arab landowner. The Knights of St John had been established as a crusading order a short time previously in Jerusalem. Historians are not entirely in agreement about whether Aqua Bella was used by a tax collector of the Order and as a place of refuge for pilgrims to Jerusalem, or if it served, at least for a time, as a nunnery.

The small castle, measuring 30 by 40 metres, had outer walls up to 12 metres high and was surrounded by a moat. It consisted of two separate courtyard castles of different heights, so that its defenders had a height advantage if they lost the lower section and had to retreat to the taller part. Aqua Bella was therefore one of the last fortresses held by Christians in the Holy Land to fall into the hands of the Muslims. Sultan Saladin did not succeed in taking it until he had a tunnel dug beneath the outer walls in 1187.

In the carefully restored ruins, the commander's house and the vaults in which animals and grain were kept are clearly visible. Since 1994, sculptures by Yigal Tomarkin linking modern art with archaeology have been placed on the site.

Address En Hemed National Park, Jerusalem 9195000, +972 2 5342741 | **Getting there** National route 1 towards Tel Aviv, En Hemed exit, almost right by the highway, follow the signs | **Hours** Summer, Sat–Thu 8am–5pm, Fri 9am–4pm; winter, Sat–Thu 8am–4pm, Fri 8am–3pm | **Tip** The white church of Notre Dame de l'Arche d'Alliance in Abu Gosh was built in 1924 on a hillside on the site of a 5th-century Byzantine church. Remains of a floor mosaic are still visible. The famous feature is the statue of the Virgin Mary on the roof.

3__ The Armenian Bar

Drinks in a thousand-year-old Crusader monastery

The Armenian Tavern, a cellar bar in the heart of the Armenian quarter between the Jaffa Gate and the Dormition Abbey, is something like a little museum with its richly adorned antique furniture, ceramics and vases, magnificent oil paintings, mirrors and chandeliers. But it also serves a remarkable range of Armenian culinary specialities such as 'lachmanjun', a kind of Armenian pizza, and 'basturma', a dried spiced meat. There is a well-stocked bar, that naturally includes Armenian liqueurs. A glass case contains rare and delicious types of arak, an aniseed spirit, although not all of these are available for customers.

In the 1990s the Aslanian family had to fight many a battle with the authorities before they were allowed to open their bar in the cellar vaults of a 1,000-year-old Crusader monastery. To furnish it, they purchased Armenian antiques and works of art in places all over the world in order to create a tavern that is truly unique. The bar and restaurant receive frequent visits from worthies and clerics of the Armenian Christian congregation, which was established in Jerusalem no less than 16 centuries ago. Many Christians arrived during the genocide against Armenians in 1917, fleeing from Turkey to Jerusalem.

The early presence in the city of the Armenian Apostolic Church is also one of the reasons why it is among the three Christian churches that bears responsibility for the Church of the Holy Sepulchre, the most important Christian place of worship in the Holy City. The Armenians in Jerusalem are regarded as keeping themselves to themselves, partly because the trauma of Turkish genocide more than 100 years ago is particularly fresh in the memory of the Armenian community here. This is hardly apparent at all in the tavern, which gives visitors an opportunity to enjoy the hospitality, the specialities and the love of life of the Armenian people.

Address 79 Armenian Patriarchate Road, Jerusalem 9191141, +972 2 6273854 | **Getting there** From the Jaffa Gate take the first road on the right, past David's Tower and take the steps down (not suitable for people with mobility difficulties) | **Hours** Tue–Sun 11am–10.30pm | **Tip** The Edward and Helen Mardigian Museum displays a fine collection of artefacts such as liturgical items, frescoes and texts on the history and culture of the Armenian people. The museum occupies an attractive building with a colonnaded courtyard (daily 9.30am–4.30pm, 79 Armenian Patriarchate Road, +972 2 6273854).

4 __ Armon Hanatziv Promenade

A survey of 3,000 years of history

There are many high-up places from which you can look down on Jerusalem – but the Armon Hanatziv Promenade is the only one with a view of more than the Old City or one district of the city. Here you have a sweeping panorama from the modern suburbs and the historic sites of the Old City and the Mount of Olives across to the Hebrew University on Mount Scopus, to Arab villages, the desert of Judaea, and on clear days even as far as the mountains by the Dead Sea. This promenade in the Talpiot district takes its name from the Hebrew term for what was once the residence of the British high commissioner. Today, the headquarters of the United Nations are situated here.

The two-kilometre-long promenade on the chain of hills south of the Old City is lit after dark by many lamps, whose design corresponds to the illumination of the King David Hotel and the YMCA building. At dusk, especially, the view of the domes, towers and walls of the Old City is breathtaking. The route, which is popular with joggers, Segway riders and cyclists, has many observation terraces and consists of three parts. Haas Promenade, some parts of which resemble a well-tended park, leads past modern buildings adorned with round arches whose architecture takes up stylistic elements of the ancient aqueduct to Jerusalem.

The hilly path along the Sherover Promenade, where old gravestones and the ruins of an aqueduct are to be seen, has many steps. It passes the thick walls of the nunnery of the 'Poor Clares', a strict religious order devoted solely to prayer, whose members, extremely unforthcoming in speech and removed from secular life, seldom leave their convent. At the end of this section is a large, attractive orchard with pomegranate and fig trees. The third and most recent section is Goldman Promenade, from where there is a wonderful view of the Old City in a number of places.

Address Daniel Yanofsky Street, Jerusalem 9381306 | Getting there Bus 12, 78 or 107 to Daniel Yanofsky Street/HaAskan Street | Tip Abu Tor, several kilometres away, is one of the few quarters of Jerusalem with a mixed Arab and Jewish population. Here you find many restaurants, cafés and galleries as well as cinemas where films are screened even on the Shabbat.

5__ The Artists' House

The dream of the Israeli avant-garde

Young artists who have set their sights high are usually very happy to get an exhibition here: Jerusalem Artists' House is regarded as the first step on the road to recognition, an ideal launch-pad into Israel's difficult art market, where countless talented people compete with each other for recognition. To get permission to work and exhibit here, they need the consent of the operator of the Artists' House and of the association of painters and sculptors in Jerusalem.

The stone building, erected in 1890 by the Ottomans in the heavy style typical of that period, used to house the Bezalel National Museum, the predecessor of the Israel Museum, and the Israeli national art school, now the Bezalel Academy for Arts and Design. Since 1965 the old house in the Nahlaot district has been home to the Association for Jerusalem Artists, which has turned it into an extremely vibrant venue for contemporary art, where many jazz concerts and talks are also held. Young artists use the attractive rooms as an art laboratory and a centre for solo or group exhibitions. Visitors can watch the painters, photographers, graphic artists, sculptors and installation artists at work.

The exhibitions, which change several times a year, present young avant-garde artists from Israel, but also from abroad. There are also retrospectives by established artists. A high-end gallery and a very successful restaurant are also based here. The Hanagid Gallery is now one of the leading galleries in Israel. It displays works by both the artists of the moment and up-and-coming youngsters that can be bought at relatively low prices.

The popular gourmet restaurant Mona is also on the premises. This elegant eatery, on the ground floor of the Artists' House, has a well-stocked bar and a crackling open fire in winter. A few tables for diners are placed outside in the pretty garden.

Address 12 Shmuel Hanagid, Jerusalem 9270200, +972 2 6253653, www.art.org.il | **Getting there** Bus 7, 9, 17 or 19 to Bezalel / Trumpeldor | **Hours** Mon, Wed, Thu 10am – 6pm, Tue 2 – 8pm, Fri 10am – 1pm, Sat 11am – 2pm; gallery: Mon 4 – 7pm, Tue 11am – 1pm & 4 – 8pm, Wed & Thu 10am – 1pm & 4 – 7pm, Fri 10am – 1pm, Sat 11am – 2pm | **Tip** Agripas 12, about 400 metres away, is a gallery, a private cooperative of 18 artists that aims to create an international artists' network as a counterweight to the commercial art market. There are changing exhibitions monthly, talks and discussions (12 Agripas Street, Mon – Thu 4.30 – 7.30pm, Fri & Sat 11am – 2pm, www.agripas12gallery.com).

6 The Artists' Village
Studios in the biblical surroundings of Ein Kerem

The picturesque village of Ein Kerem in the idyllic hilly scenery of Judaea is many-sided. It is an important place for Christian pilgrims and attractive for tourists who are looking for galleries, studios and pretty places to eat and drink. Being close to Jerusalem, it is also a popular destination for day trips, especially on the Shabbat, because many shops and restaurants are then open here. Well-off Israelis have made their homes in the green valley at the foot of Mount Orah. Before Israel became independent, most of the residents here were Arabs, but few of them now remain.

In the winding lanes of the village with its blooming gardens are many small workshops and studios. The doors are often open, as many artists and craftspeople are happy for visitors to watch them at work – and of course they sell what they make. A small map with the addresses of 18 artists is available. 'Ein Kerem', meaning 'spring of the vineyard', is seldom overcrowded. The atmosphere is relaxed and intimate. At weekends, concerts of chamber music are held in the Eden-Tamir Music Center.

The quiet village also has great historical significance. It is the birthplace of John the Baptist. The Church of St John, in which is situated the cave where he was born, is named after him. It occupies the spot where, according to a legend, the mothers of John and Jesus, Elizabeth and Mary, once met. Mary is said to have refreshed herself here at a spring. Today, pilgrims fill their drinking bottles with holy water from this 'Well of the Virgin'. Here and there, among palm trees, cedars, fig trees and almond trees, the towers of several monasteries, but above all the golden domes of the Russian Al Moscobia Monastery, rise above the village idyll. In Ein Kerem there are also important traces of Jewish history, for example ruins from the time of Herod and a 2,000-year-old mikvah, a ritual Jewish bath.

Address Ein Kerem 9087200 | Getting there Tram to the last stop, Mount Herzl, then bus 28 | Tip The Franciscan Monastery of St John in the Desert is three kilometres to the west. In a cave that now shelters a small chapel, John the Baptist is said to have retreated into solitude to prepare himself for his mission.

7__Avital Car Hotel

Sleep in an Oldsmobile

It is two-star accommodation with only 12 rooms and does not really stand out. The rooms are pleasant and comfortable by the standards of a small, basic hotel. But for visitors to Jerusalem who love cars and their history, Avital in its narrow, four-storey building is a tip for insiders. Where else can you sleep in a bed with a frame made from a veteran Lincoln? Or converse about matters of mutual interest with a person who has profound knowledge of historic car models and collects them, and who sometimes eye-catchingly parks his bright yellow Maserati sports car or a veteran automobile on the pavement as an advertisement?

In close proximity to the picturesque Mahane Yehuda Market, in 1992 Nitzan Avital fulfilled his dream of opening a friendly apartment hotel with a welcoming atmosphere, at the same time dedicating it to his great hobby: cars. More than 400 model cars from all over the world are exhibited in the window displays and glass cases of the small hotel lobby, which simultaneously acts as the reception area and breakfast room. Some of the small old-time cars such as the models of a Ford T Tourer from 1912 or a Reo Touring from 1917 cost several hundred euros at auctions. In the breakfast room, which is used as a café in the daytime, international specialist journals about veteran cars lie around for interested guests.

However, the hotel, now run by Nitzan's sons Ziv and Izkik, became famous in Israel not only for these valuable models. When Nitzan, who was born in Poland, described his tough, stubborn and ultimately successful battle against cancer in two books, he became a role model and a source of encouragement for many Israelis. In 2012, he received the citizens' prize of the city of Jerusalem for his life's work. Nitzan Avital has a loyal following on social networks and was received by Israel's prime minister Benjamin Netanyahu.

Address 141 Jaffa Street, Jerusalem 9434241, +972 2 6243706, www.avitalhotel.co.il | Getting there Tram to Mahane Yehuda | Tip Restaurant Machneyuda, one of the city's best and most spectacular restaurants, gains plaudits for its ambitious cross-over cuisine at prices to match, but even more for its atmosphere. The cooks and waiters often sing Israeli songs or popular hits at the top of their voices, and people dance on the tables (Beit Ya'akov Street 10, +972 2 5333442, Sun–Thu 12.30pm–midnight, 4–6.30pm closed, Fri 11.30am–3pm, Sat 6.30pm–midnight).

8 — The Baidun Gallery

Buying archaeological finds legally

Everyone in the shuk, the bazaar of the Old City, knows the branch of the Baidun Gallery in the Via Dolorosa. But not many people know that Khader M. Baidun, the present head of an old-established family of traders in artefacts, also has a workshop and store just round the corner. If you ask in the branches, they are usually pleased to direct you there.

The archaeological treasures piled up here seem to exist in enormous quantities in the Holy City. Roman coins, Greek vases, Phoenician bracelets, Israelite pottery jars and Persian daggers are sold as antiques in many shops in Jerusalem. Healthy mistrust about the authenticity of the items is appropriate, and in particular it is advisable to check you have papers allowing them to be exported legally. It is not unusual for the jewellery, the ceramic pots, glasses or spearheads to derive from illegal excavations. There are severe penalties for buying and exporting these.

The Baidun family, who have been dealing in antiques for more than 90 years, have a state licence and a good reputation, although they too have been in the sights of the Israeli antiques office in the past. But anyone who, like the Baiduns, possesses such a great quantity of ancient items, dating from the times of the Canaanites, Israelites and Mesopotamians through to the Byzantine and Ottoman periods, sometimes has difficulties in explaining their provenance. To get an impression of this, visit the Baiduns' premises and picturesque courtyard.

If you are lucky, Khadar Baidun will offer a small glass of tea and talk about past prominent customers such as the Israeli war hero Moshe Dayan or delegates from the Vatican, and then let you look in the overflowing antiques warehouse, parts of which are not arranged in any order. All of the artefacts together have a total value of at least 100 million US dollars, the owner believes.

Address 19, 20 & 28 Via Dolorosa, Jerusalem 91440, +972 54 7371066, www.baidun.com | **Getting there** From the Damascus Gate go along El Wad Street, then left to the Via Dolorosa | **Hours** Daily 10am–6pm | **Tip** The Holy Sepulchre Store is a shop in the Christian Quarter that stocks an abundance of religious items for the Greek Orthodox community. Here you can buy valuable icons and exclusive jewellery – though the owner, Nicolas Elias, is not pleased to see tourists who have no interest in buying anything in his fine shop (49 Christian Quarter Road).

9 Begin's Monument

Memorial to a radical Zionist

The Menachem Begin Heritage Center traces the dramatic history of Israel through the life story of the former prime minister Begin (1913–1992). Photographs, documents, flyers, weapons and furniture, complemented by multimedia presentations, historic film footage and recordings of music and speech, take visitors on a dense, sensual, sometimes disturbing journey through decades of war.

Begin's biography is dominated by his political and military struggle for a strong Israel. After studying law, he became a Zionist activist in Poland and Czechoslovakia, fled from the Nazis, was taken prisoner by the Soviets and condemned as an 'agent'. In 1942, he escaped to Palestine. Begin became head of the underground organisation Irgun, which fought against the forces of the British Mandate. Irgun was responsible for the terrorist attack on the King David Hotel in 1946, which killed 81 people, and an alleged massacre of Arabs in Deir Yassin in 1948. Reports of these events are contradictory: the Zionists claimed to have given the hotel several advance warnings of the attack. The British vehemently denied this. The Israelis dispute that a massacre took place during the fighting in Deir Yassin.

After independence in 1948, Begin was one of Israel's leading right-wing politicians. His study has been reconstructed in the Heritage Center, which also runs lectures, cultural events and discussions (often in English). Begin's radicalism made him a controversial figure at all times – and the Heritage Center does not conceal this. Jewish intellectuals such as Hannah Arendt and Albert Einstein called Begin's Herut Party terrorist and racist. However, in 1978, as prime minister, Begin made peace with President Muhammad Anwar al-Sadat of Egypt through the mediation of the American president Jimmy Carter, and returned the occupied Sinai. Both received the Nobel Peace Prize for this.

Address 6 Sh. A. Nakhon Street, Jerusalem 9411014, +972 2 5652020, www.begincenter.org.il | Getting there Bus 7, 18, 34 or 77 to Menachem Begin Heritage Center | Hours Sun, Mon, Wed & Thu 9am–4.30pm, Tue 9am–7pm, Fri 9am–12.30pm | Tip The Ketef Hinnom Archaeological Museum is round the corner. It holds two silver rolls in Old Hebrew script from the 7th century BCE, the oldest extant written evidence of Bible-related texts (1 David Remez Street, Sun–Thu 10am–6pm, Fri 10am–12.30pm).

10__The Beit Alliance

Arts centre and a tip for parties

The 'Alliance House', once a school and for a time refugee accommodation, is one of Jerusalem's historic edifices that has become an arts centre. This square-looking building dating from 1880 next to Mahane Yehuda Market is a venue for working, debating and partying. Filmmakers, musicians, designers and dancers attend workshops here, but amateurs, visitors and tourists are welcome as guests. The talks and courses are often held in English.

Beit Alliance is above all an exciting, vibrant place for young creative people. Writers, sculptors, fashion designers, musicians and multimedia artists have their studios here. Small high-tech start-ups and a dance ensemble are also among the tenants. There is even a barbershop. Exhibitions present the works of the Alliance artists. For performances and concerts there is a hall, and also the large courtyard. And the Alliance parties, often held on Thursdays, have a legendary reputation as wild and thrilling events.

In 2015, a businessman bought the premises to open a boutique hotel, but in the face of a time-consuming approval process he handed over the run-down building to New Spirit, a non-profit initiative that since 2003 has worked to stop the outward flow of non-religious residents from Jerusalem: every year more than 1,000 citizens, mostly young, move to Tel Aviv, which is less dominated by the orthodox, for example on the Shabbat, than the Holy City.

To make Jerusalem more attractive for secular Israelis, a large team from New Spirit gives diverse support to young people in the arts and founders of pubs and companies, creating social networks, places of encounter and cooperations. This highly successful initiative, which is supported by the Israeli government, is funded by subsidies and donations from the city government, many companies, foundations and organisations in Israel and other countries.

Address 5 Ki'akh Street, Jerusalem 93542, www.new-spirit.org.il/en/alliance-house and on Facebook: Beit Alliance | **Getting there** Tram to Mahane Yehuda F; bus 17, 18, 19 or 66 to Nevi'im | **Tip** The Muslala Art Collective, a local initiative for arts and ecology, is on the fifth floor of the Clal Center, where you see political art and posters on the walls, as well as a fish pond, an organic beehive and experimental crop planting on the large roof terrace (97 Jaffa Road).

11__Beit Shmuel
Insights into the Jewish world

For visitors from abroad, Jerusalem's lively theatre scene is of little use, as the Hebrew language is a barrier to understanding. The Hirsch Theatre, where plays and musicals are staged in English, is an exception. The theatre is part of Beit Shmuel – Mercas Shimshon, the cultural, educational and administrative complex of the World Union for Progressive Judaism. This headquarters of the organisation of liberal Jews, which has 1.8 million members, most of them in the USA, is situated only a few hundred metres from the bastion of orthodox Jews in Mea Shearim.

In Judaism, they form a counterweight to the ultra-orthodox. Liberal Jews believe that Judaism must adapt to modern times without abandoning its cultural identity. The headquarters of the organisation in Mishkenot Shaanamin, the first Jewish settlement outside the city walls, is of interest to non-Jewish visitors. The old building, dating from 1986, with its rooms for courses, offices, a canteen and bedrooms right next to the Hirsch Theatre, has a beautifully planted green courtyard with a café. The second complex of buildings is home to the Blaustein Hall, designed by award-winning architect Moshe Safdie, with its spectacular glass construction, a hotel and further spaces for the organisation's ambitious arts programme. It provides an exciting insight into modern Jewish life and thinking. Here, too, many of the events are held in English, as Jews living abroad are an important group to be addressed.

The topics of the performances, readings and panel discussions are often the dramas of the 20th century: the horror of the Holocaust, the Jewish underground struggle against the British, conflicts with the Arabs, the endeavours of the Jewish state to find its identity between religious orthodoxy and socialist visions. However, the programme also includes entertaining concerts, dance performances and cabaret.

Address Hirsch Theatre: 13 King David Street, Jerusalem 9410806; congress and hotel centre: 6 Eliyahu Shema Street, Jerusalem 9410806, +972 2 6203455, www.beitshmuel.com/en-us, www.wupj.org/beit-shmuel-mercaz-shimshon | Getting there Bus 13, 18, 49 or 78 to David HaMelekh/Hess | Tip Rooftop, in the luxury hotel Mamilla, is a first-class restaurant with a long bar and party tables. From up here you have a superb view of all Jerusalem (Mamilla Hotel, King Solomon Street 11, Jerusalem 94182, +972 2 5482230, Sun–Thu 6–11pm, Fri noon–4pm, after this only a Shabbat menu, Sat noon–9.30pm Shabbat menu, then normal menu until 11pm).

12 Bet Hansen

Artistic meeting place in the old lepers' colony

In Jerusalem, where there are over 80 museums and many ambitious festivals take place every year, quality and originality are essential for arts institutions. Since it opened in 2013, the culture and technology centre Hansen House has gained a considerable reputation through its interdisciplinary congresses, out-of-the-ordinary concerts, bold events such as a backgammon tournament for Jews and Arabs, workshops, lectures and many art projects.

The centre, which is open to the public free of charge, is a hip place to meet for young people. The extensive garden serves as an exhibition space for art objects and installations, as a market for works by artists and designers, sometimes as a studio, and as a rendezvous for students of arts and information technology. The Bezalel Design Academy uses Bet Hansen as a place for experimenting with new media. Many works of art that were created here have received a lot of attention. The art project The Eternal Sukkah, a hut of branches for the Sukkot festival made from a Bedouin house, was purchased by the Israel Museum in 2015.

For the Centre for Design, Media and Technology it is advantageous to be based in a historic building in the high-class district of Talbiya. Until the year 2000 it was a nursing home for people suffering from leprosy. Funded by a German baroness, Augusta von Keffenbrink-Ascheraden, and designed by the famous German missionary and architect Conrad Schick, the two-storey, severely symmetrical building complex with its spacious courtyard was inaugurated in 1867. Leprosy was still incurable at that time. From 1887, the refuge for lepers was run by Protestant communities, until in 1950 the Israeli state took it over. A permanent multimedia exhibition about the history of the institution can be found in the heritage-listed building, which has a shaded walkway above the courtyard on the first floor.

Address 14 Gedalyahu Alon Street, Jerusalem 93555, +972 2 5973702, www.hansen.co.il, www.facebook.com/hansen.house.1887 | Getting there Bus 18 or 74 to the Jerusalem Theatre | Hours Sun–Thu 10am–6pm, Fri 10am–2pm | Tip Less than 300 metres away, the Natural History Museum occupied a lovely 19th-century building surrounded by a charming sculpture garden with exhibitions on themes related to zoology and natural history (6 Mohaliver Street, German Colony, Sun, Tue, Thu 9am–2pm, Mon & Wed 6–7pm, Sat 10am–2pm).

13__ The Bethesda Cistern

For miraculous healing

Columns, steps, the plans of halls and water basins identifiable by passages and walls – this site of ruins, almost as large as two football pitches, conveys an idea of the determination with which buildings were raised here in ancient times, then were reduced to rubble and ashes, and then reconstructed again and again. Here, archaeologists found the remains of a large Jewish pool, a Roman sanctuary and steam bath, an Islamic school and two churches, which were destroyed several times.

The oldest traces show that, in about 200 BCE, there was a large pool, cut up to 15 metres deep from the rock and surrounded by four colonnades, each 9 metres tall. Built right across the ensemble was a fifth colonnade, to divide the water basins. They were used by Jewish high priests for ritual ablutions in the temple. Evidence of this pool was not found until after 1888, when French monks discovered steps leading to a cistern, 120 metres long and 60 metres wide, divided several times over, near St Anne's Church. This find had great significance for Christians, as the site is regarded as a place where Jesus performed miracles. According to John the Evangelist, Christ healed a lame man at the pool of Bethesda. However, for a long time there was no sign of a pool in this place.

After the destruction of Jerusalem in 70 CE, the Romans built a sanctuary to Aesculapius – the Greek god of health and medicine – and a steam bath here. About the year 500, the Byzantines erected a great basilica, which the Persians destroyed some 100 years later. Christians rebuilt it shortly afterwards. In 1009, Sultan Al-Hakim razed this church to the ground; 150 years later Crusaders built a small church on the spot, which was converted to an Islamic school by Sultan Saladin. The structure fell into decay until it was restored, again as a church and dedicated to St Anne, in the mid-19th century.

Address Burj Laqlaq Strat, Jerusalem 91194, +972 2 6251515 | **Getting there** Bus 1, 3 or 83a to Jericho Road/HaFaoel Road, entrance to the Old City via the Lion Gate | **Tip** The Lion Gate with its exit to the Mount of Olives, built by Suleiman the Magnificent in the 16th century, had great strategic significance in the Six-Day War, as the Israeli soldiers entered the Old City here. The gate takes its name from the reliefs of two panthers on the outer side of the city wall that were popularly thought to be lions.

14_The Bezalel Market

Niche art sales and delicatessen

Art markets are not usually found among cafés, ice cream parlours and bars. But when people stroll around the Bezalel artists' market, the stall owners have to compete with the temptations offered by many other places on the street that have put out tables and chairs, shaded by big parasols. However, the quiet Bezalel market, held on Fridays in two small, traffic-free lanes, attracts customers with some highly original items. Large sunshades stop the scorching sun from driving away passing trade. In bad, cold or rainy weather, the market is sometimes called off.

Artists and craftspeople, most of them young, sit at improvised little stands to sell works in fabric, drawings, paintings, carvings, sculptures, glass creations, ceramics, leather goods, blankets, scarves and clothes. But there are also professional producers selling unusual clocks, kitchen utensils, decorative items, jewellery, toys, dolls, lamps, Judaica and children's clothing made from a wide range of materials. Farmers from the region sell fine spirits that they have distilled themselves, sometimes from exotic fruits, as well as organic wines, juice, baked goods, honey products, different kinds of oil, vinegar and herbs, and natural cosmetics.

The Bezalel Artists' Market was set up in 2009 on the initiative of some gallery owners and with support from the city authorities of Jerusalem, who want to further upgrade this district with its numerous arts institutions, galleries and little designer shops. The market long ago ceased to sell only art and craft products. The project close to the old Bezalel Academy of Arts and Design quickly became a hit with locals and tourists. Solo singers, bands and street performers now often appear on market days. However, the atmosphere is not crowded or hectic, which may be a result of the relatively high prices of the items sold here.

Address Shats Street and Bezalel Street, Jerusalem 9426702, +972 52 4794141, www.facebook.com/bezalel.fair | Getting there Bus 7, 19, 75 or 78 to Bezalel / Trumpeldor | Hours Winter, Fri 9am – 3pm; summer, Fri 10am – 4pm | Tip The lively Ben Yehuda pedestrian zone, less than 300 metres from the Bezalel market, has a colourful mix of souvenir and clothes stores, stands with kippahs bearing logos of sports clubs from all over the world, and old-fashioned shops selling Judaica, arts & crafts and knick-knacks, ice cream parlours, hamburger and falafel stands. Buskers often play here.

15__ The Bird Observatory

An idyllic view of migratory and exotic birds

The Jerusalem Bird Observatory has an unusually significant site. It lies in park-like landscape that is also the location of the Israeli parliament, the supreme court and the residence of the prime minister. An advantage of this well-guarded situation in the extensive Sacher Park is that it is generally quiet and free of construction work. Ornithologists appreciate this, even though in 1995 the state allocated no more than half a hectare, about 5,000 square metres, for their work.

This bird observatory in Jerusalem is one of six centres in Israel for watching birds. Although a small country, Israel is an important stop-over station for migratory birds flying in from Europe and western Asia. Each year, millions of storks, eagles, buzzards, nightingales, swallows, robins and swifts cross through Israel on their north-south route, and have excellent conditions for a short stay in its densely vegetated landscape with a relatively large number of bodies of water.

At the observatory in Jerusalem you can also see native bird species such as the hoopoe, Israel's national bird, owls, the short-eared eagle and the Palestine sunbird. Some endangered birds can be found nesting nearby in the spring. There has been a modest boom in tourism in Israel through bird-watchers from all over the world. The data that are collected here about the migratory birds are important for scientific purposes, not only for ornithologists but also for researchers on climate and the environment.

The Jerusalem Bird Observatory, which includes an aviary, is not the most important one in Israel but it enables visitors to enjoy an extremely varied programme. For example, even when the experts put rings on birds there is an opportunity for the public to watch and join in. As well as watching birds, tourists, both adults and children, can take part in various workshops, night walks and excursions.

Address Jerusalem Bird Observatory, Sacher Park, Jerusalem, +972 2 6537374 | Getting there Bus 9, 24 or 99 to Knesset | Hours Accessible 24 hours | Tip The Gail Rubin Gallery is a permanent exhibition, part of the bird observatory complex, showing works by photographers and artists looking at the fauna and flora of Israel from various points of view (Sun–Thu 9am–3pm).

16 Borderline
Palestinian garden restaurants

A recommendation by *The New York Times* for restaurants in East Jerusalem is unusual. But Borderline and the neighbouring Pasha have been, alongside the legendary American Colony, the traditional rendezvous for Palestinians, diplomats, staff of non-governmental organisations and media correspondents for more than 20 years. East and West meet in a restored Arab villa, as *The Jerusalem* Post wrote.

Both garden restaurants, with several rooms colourfully decorated in the Arab style in the high-class residential district of Sheikh Jarrah, belong to the Shawan family. In their popular, sometimes extremely crowded eateries, all meals are prepared with fresh and original ingredients and spices, they emphasise. They attach importance to the fact that Israelis from West Jerusalem, too, are welcome guests. For orthodox Jews, however, these Arab restaurants, specialising in Middle Eastern dishes with lamb and chicken, all kinds of skilfully spiced mezze starters, fine stews, flatbread baked on the premises and honey-soaked desserts would scarcely be acceptable.

Although Muslims and Jews to some extent have similar rules about food, for example the fact that both religions strictly abjure pork, kosher food differs clearly from halal dishes. One of the best-known specialities of Pasha, mansaf, has been considered since time immemorial as nothing less than a provocation for adherents of Jewish dietary rules, which are absolutely opposed to mixing meat and dairy products. Mansaf, however, is a small lamb, slowly cooked in fermented yoghurt – a great delicacy for many people, but taboo for Jews.

For those who wish to round off the meal here by smoking an oriental hookah, there is a choice between many kinds of sweet tobacco. The music in the restaurants is sometimes very loud, and there is also dancing – something untypical in a Muslim environment.

Address 13 Shimon Hazadiq Street, Jerusalem 9725013, +972 2 5825162 (Pasha), +972 2 5328342 (Borderline), www.facebook.com/pg/borderlineofjerusalem, www.borderlinerestaurant.com, www.pashasofjerusalem.com | Getting there Tram, bus 17, 201, 207, 254, 273 or 274 to Shim'on Ha Tsadik | Hours Sun–Wed noon–1am, Thu noon–6pm (sometimes until 2am) | Tip The Orient House has belonged to the prestigious Al-Husseini family since 1897 and has seen high-ranking visitors, including emperors: Wilhelm II of Germany in 1898 and Haile Selassie of Ethiopia in 1936. From 1983 it was the PLO headquarters, but was closed in 2001 by the Israeli authorities after the suicide attack in Pizzeria Sbarro (8 Abu Ubaida Street).

17__The Burnt House

A glimpse of everyday life 2,000 years ago

The story behind this building is spectacular. The museum is an extremely interesting opportunity to gain an impression of what life may have been like in Jerusalem 2,000 years ago. Although the exhibits only amount to a few artefacts, at the heart of the museum a fascinating film shows what has been discovered in and beneath the building. The ruins of the house of the Katros family, who were the high priests at the time of the Second Temple, were uncovered in 1970. Visitors cannot, however, enter the excavations.

This sensational archaeological site consists of the foundation walls of the house, which have survived to a height of one metre. Researchers found them beneath a layer of ash six metres thick. The entrance hall, four rooms, a small kitchen and a basin for ritual ablutions have been identified. During the excavations, a Roman spear, water vessels, ink pots, coins, a kitchen mortar and household items were found, as well as the arm bones of a young woman. According to scientific investigation they were buried according to Jewish rites. Some of the finds seem to confirm, almost 2,000 years later, the accusation made in the Talmud that Katros was a fraudster: falsely marked weights were found.

The dramatically made film, lasting nearly 30 minutes with a soundtrack in Hebrew, English, Spanish or French, describes the last days in the house of this family of priests in the reign of King Herod. Against the background of the fighting between Jewish rebels and Romans after the destruction of the Second Temple in 70 CE, the family have heated arguments about the issues of violence, resistance and self-defence. Then Roman soldiers set fire to the house. The proof that the family of the high priests of the temple lived here is a large stone bearing an inscription in Aramaic that lay in the ruins: 'Bar Katros' (son of Katros).

מוזיאון הבית השרוף בית קטרוס

THE BURNT HOUSE MUSEUM – BEIT KATROS

Address 2 Tiferet Yisrael Road, Jerusalem 9752268, +972 2 6265906 | Getting there
Enter the Jewish Quarter from the Jaffa Gate or the Damascus Gate | **Hours** Sun
10am–5pm, Mon–Thu 9am–5pm, Fri 9am–1pm | **Tip** The Isaac Kaplan Old Yishuv
Court Museum, in a building that has been used by Jews for 500 years, is dedicated to
the life of the Jewish population from 1800 to 1948. It shows the living conditions in
the Old City (6 Or Ha-Haim Street, Sun–Thu 10am–5pm, Fri 10am–1pm).

18_ Caliber 3

Anti-terror drill for professionals and tourists

If you want to learn from the professionals how to defend yourself against criminals and terrorists, you can expect a challenge. The Israeli Counter Terror and Security Academy, based in the hills south of Jerusalem, offers this unusual opportunity: anyone can take part in its training courses. But even during the two-hour introductory workshop you have to be prepared to do press-ups and practise shooting.

The instructors are experienced military officers, who train many thousands of bodyguards, police officers and armed forces personnel from all over the world every year. With the encouragement of the Israeli government, Colonel Sharon Gat, a former member of the Israeli Defence Forces (IDF), has set up four anti-terror training centres in Israel since 2003 – and there is a branch of Caliber 3 in San Diego in the USA. The courses for security professionals last between a week and three months. Civilians and tourists can book courses lasting up to a week in this Jewish settlement on the West Bank – at prices that run to several thousand euros.

The programme comprehends courses in the Israeli martial art Krav Maga (which combines judo, karate and boxing), workshops for shooting pistols and rifles using live ammunition, and survival training. But the activities also include climbing and paintball training at a higher level than normal wargames played for fun. Some of the courses are specially for children and young people.

Caliber 3 sets its sights high. Its purpose is not only to teach the ability to fight, but also to demonstrate the determination of the Israelis to defend themselves with maximum efficiency and high moral standards, states Colonel Gat. After all, following the tragedy for the Jewish people in the Holocaust, it is something of a miracle that the whole world wants to learn from Israel, of all states, how to defend itself against terrorism.

Address Gush Etzion Industrial Park, Gush Etzion 29173, +972 2 6734334, www.caliber3range.com | Getting there From Jerusalem take national route 60 for about 13 kilometres south to Gush Etzion. Caliber 3 is at the end of the settlement – follow the signs; by bus from Jerusalem, information +972 2 6734334; bus 167 or 169 to Gush Etzion Industrial Park | Hours Sun–Fri by arrangement | Tip If you like shooting as harmless fun, go to Space Laser for a battle with laser light weapons (1 Azaria Street, Emek Refaim district, +972 2 9663535, Sun–Wed 11am–11pm, Thu 11am–3am, Fri 10am–2pm).

19___Carousela

A living room for many foreign students

The corner café has the bohemian charm of a lovingly fitted student's room, with striking pictures, lots of books, posters and a colourful mix of furniture and lamps. The clientele in Carousela consists of young people, students, lecturers and staff of the nearby university, institutes and cultural organisations. A particularly large number of students from abroad love this unconventional café in the friendly district of Rechavia.

The quarter has been described as 'Grunewald in the Orient', because many German Jews, especially from Berlin where the district of Grunewald is located, found a common refuge here in the 1930s. Today, Rechavia with its parks and well-kept houses is a coveted, quiet and by no means cheap residential area. Many small shops, restaurants, bars and cafés bring some life to this otherwise tranquil quarter. At its heart, however is Smolenski Street, short and closed to traffic, the site of the heavily guarded private residence of the Israeli prime minister.

Like many places to eat in Israel, Carousela no longer serves meat and fish dishes, but the specialities, which change daily, are much praised: vegetarian stews, pies and pasta dishes. 'Alternative kosher' is how Jonathan Vadel, the café owner, describes his cuisine, which includes an opulent selection for breakfast, salads, sandwiches and cake. Vadel is one of the rebellious café and restaurant proprietors in Jerusalem who, in 2012, opposed the monopoly of the orthodox chief rabbinate in awarding seals for kosher food. They were successful in campaigning for a municipally controlled authority, which is now responsible for the certificate. Sometimes the café, which has a few tables outside, is transformed into a little bazaar for craft producers or fashion designers. Singers and bands often perform in the evenings, when it gets crowded, as the space is limited.

Address 1 Binyamin mi-Tudela Street, Jerusalem 92305, +972 2 6505024, www.facebook.com/
Carousela | Getting there Bus 9, 17, 19, 22, 32, 267 or 791 to Azza Street / Radak Street |
Hours Sat – Thu 8am – midnight, Fri 8am – 3pm | Tip Bonem House nearby is among the
most attractive German-style buildings in Rehavia. It is a structure of interlocking volumes
and large, pale-coloured surfaces with horizontal windows and a floor mosaic, designed by the
Bauhaus architect Leopold Krakauer for a doctor's family in 1935 (21 Ramban Street).

20__ The Cellar Bar

Politics and drinks in the American Colony

The American Colony Hotel lives and breathes history to this day. For almost 100 years, this small, stylish luxury hotel has been a rare place of neutrality for the various rulers of the city, for changing occupying forces and regional power holders, for opponents from political, ethnic and religious groups. This architectural jewel in the Arab east of the city delights visitors with its well-tended gardens, fountains and enchanting courtyards, with a multitude of columns and arches, mosaics and thick Persian carpets, as well as the spacious rooms in which a rich Turkish businessman once resided with his four wives.

Nowhere is the mix of history and politics headier than down in the low-vaulted Cellar Bar. In this intimate basement space with its old-fashioned furnishings and warm pink stone floor, you can even order a Taybe beer, brewed by Christian Palestinians – as well as all the classic cocktails. Old photographs illustrating a wealth of history hang on the walls. The bar seats have been occupied by such famous people as Winston Churchill, Marc Chagall, Tony Blair, Leon Uris, John Le Carré and Lawrence of Arabia. This traditional rendezvous for diplomats and correspondents, Palestinians and Israelis, settlers and big landowners, for high-ranking representatives of the churches, the United Nations and aid organisations has lost little of its former importance. The first Israeli-Egyptian peace talks leading to the Treaty of Oslo in 1993 started here. The American Colony Hotel advertises itself as a 'neutral zone' in the Middle Eastern conflict – although a handful of other institutions and places in Jerusalem make similar claims.

The hotel is also extremely popular with couples. They are especially attracted to the romantic green courtyard. Here, generously spaced, stand tables of the restaurant, which serves acclaimed food.

Address 1 Louis Vincent Street, Jerusalem 97200, +972 2 6279777, www.americancolony.com | Getting there Bus 17, 112, 201 or 207 to Derekh Shem / Louis Vincent | Hours Daily 5.30pm–2am | Tip The complex is also home to Munther's Bookshop, one of the best English-language bookshops in the region for non-fiction (1 Louis Vincent Street, +972 2 6279777).

21 The Chagall Windows
Great art in the clinic synagogue

The Hadassah University Clinic is a hospital but also a destination for art lovers. Visitors to this huge complex, while they make their way to Marc Chagall's works, get as a side-effect an impression of the efficiency and dynamism of this famous hospital in its huge, bustling entrance lobby. You enter the Abel Synagogue through an inconspicuous wooden door. Beyond it are 12 glass-mosaic windows, each 3.40 metres high and 2.50 metres wide, by the Franco-Russian artist.

The airy rectangular synagogue with its pale wooden benches seems almost too small for the 12 large arched windows with their diverse colours. Chagall's instructions were to dedicate each window to one of the 12 sons of Jacob, the tribal patriarchs, without recognisably depicting them or any other person. The representation of persons is not permitted by the Jewish faith. The artist therefore envisaged the 12 tribes of Israel using fabulous creatures, trees, flowers and fruit, and with stars and symbolic roofs of buildings (like the domes of Jerusalem). Each of them refers to one of Jacob's blessings for his 12 sons and the blessings of Moses for the 12 tribes of Israel. For the stained-glass windows, Chagall and his assistant Charles Marc developed their own process for applying the pigments, which enabled them to use three different colours on a pane of glass without lead strips to divide them.

After two years of work, for which he charged no fee, Chagall himself handed over the windows to the Hadassah organisation in Paris in 1962 on the occasion of its 50th anniversary celebrations. He stated that it was a matter of great happiness for him to be permitted to donate the works to the Jewish people. Several windows were damaged during the Six-Day War in 1967, and later repaired by Chagall. He left a bullet hole in the green window, however, as a symbol of the horrors of war.

Address Kiryat Hadassah, Jerusalem 91120, +972 2 6776271, www.hadassah-med.com | Getting there Bus 12, 19 or 27 to Hadassah Medical Center | Hours Sun–Thu 8.30am–3.30pm | Tip Diners at the restaurant Karma in Ein Kerem have a wonderful view of pretty countryside from the tastefully furnished interior, and above all from the terrace of its small, picturesque building. Good Italian-Israeli meals are served (74 Ein Kerem, +972 2 6436643).

22__ The Chapel of Peace

A Benedictine nuns' icon for Protestants

The small Chapel of Peace in the south aisle of the Church of the Redeemer stands for a big idea. Here is located an icon, a gift by Roman Catholic Benedictine nuns on the Mount of Olives to an ecumenical church congress in 1991. This is remarkable, because in the Christian world there are traditionally few places in which ecumenical thinking meets as much resistance as in the Holy City, where the churches often quarrel over every square, every ruin and every biblical site. The icon is a reminder of Noah and the rainbow that God put in the clouds as a sign of peace with humankind. In the space reserved for meditation, with a few chairs in front of the icon, the aim is for prayers to be said for the end of fights and quarrels.

It was not until the 19th century that German Protestants discovered their devotion to Jerusalem. As interest in the city revived across Europe, Protestant Prussia began to get involved. In Muristan, near the Church of the Sepulchre, the Church of the Redeemer was built from 1869 on the ground plan of an old Crusader church. On Reformation Day 1898, the church was consecrated as a symbol of Protestant unity in the presence of Kaiser Wilhelm II. He was the first western ruler in modern times to visit the Holy City.

The repeated fighting over Jerusalem in the 20th century damaged the Church of the Redeemer several times, and the traces were removed again and again. But even in this Protestant foreign congregation, to which a pastor is sent from Germany for a few years at a time, the regional conflict is constantly present: members of the congregation live in Israel, Jordan and the Palestinian territories. The church does a lot to live up to the aim that it sets for itself: to be 'a voice for reconciliation by German-speaking Christians among the manifold political, cultural, historical and religious divisions'.

Address 5 Muristan Road, Jerusalem 91140, +972 2 6266800 | Getting there Enter the Old City through the Jaffa Gate, then go left through the Armenian Quarter and turn left into Christian Quarter Road | Hours Mon–Sat 10am–5pm, Sun only for church services | Tip The entrance to the archaeological zone Through the Ages is inside the church. Its multi-media exhibition is a trip through history to a quarry of Herod's period, gardens from the time of Jesus, buildings under Emperor Hadrian, walls of the marketplace when Emperor Constantine ruled, and the mosaic floor of the Crusader church of Santa Maria Latina.

23__ The Chords Bridge

Biblical inspiration for star architect Calatrava

Jerusalem has many world-famous monuments. The suspension bridge by the Spanish architect Santiago Calatrava, inaugurated in 2008, is regarded as the only modern landmark in the Holy City, however. Many residents were sceptical about whether this bold, futuristic structure would fit in with the numerous sacred places, ancient buildings and ruins in the city. The editor of an Israeli architectural journal criticised the spectacular bridge, which is intended to be reminiscent of a white harp, as a 'monster that represents the architect's ego and not the city of Jerusalem'.

Since then, most citizens of Jerusalem have become proud of the delicate-looking bridge, which is borne by 66 cables of white steel, hanging from a white steel mast 118 metres high. It is popularly known as 'King David's harp', the 'sail' or the 'spider's web'. In designing it, Calatrava took inspiration from the words of psalm number 150 in the Bible: 'Praise him with the sound of the trumpet: praise him with the psaltery and harp.' This made it easier for the many orthodox residents of the neighbourhood to accept this out-of-the-ordinary architecture.

The bridge cost €49 million and was mainly built for Jerusalem's (so far solitary) tram line, which has been crossing the whole city from west to east since 2011. Pedestrians, too, can use the 360-metre-long curved structure.

Originally the city authorities planned a simple concrete bridge, but eventually decided in favour of this much more expensive version in order to enhance the quality of the district, which is the crossing point of expressways. The neighbouring districts are dominated by plain modern residential blocks and hotels, and by public office buildings.

The view of Calatrava's 450-ton bridge at the western entrance to Jerusalem is especially enthralling at night, when it is illuminated in bright colours with LED effects.

Address Between Jaffa Road and Sderot Shazar Street, Jerusalem 9543502 | Getting there Tram to Central Station and Kiryat Moshe; bus 6, 66, 141, 361 or 461 to Central Station | Tip Jerusalem's central bus station, one stop from the bridge, is also a lively, somewhat old-fashioned shopping centre. In contrast to places in the tourist areas of the centre and the Old City, the prices in the shops and snack bars here are rarely exorbitant (228 Jaffa Road).

24 The Cinematheque

A cult site, not only during the film festival

There are few cinemas in the world that give such an overwhelming panoramic view. From the large terrace of this old-established picture house you can gaze upon the beautifully illuminated walls of the Old City. The Cinematheque is at the heart of the city's cultural life, not only during the annual Jerusalem Film Festival. The programmes, which constantly change, are devoted for days or weeks to a particular period of cinema, to a director or star of the screen, to the movie productions of a country or to a genre. In addition, there are live broadcasts of concerts and operas, for example from the New York Metropolitan Opera.

Films from all over the world are usually screened in the original language, sometimes with subtitles in Hebrew, in the various auditoria of the Cinematheque. The audience here, correspondingly, is international. The spacious cinema, which is decorated with numerous historic film accessories and equipment, is also a venue for events such as discussions and talks. The attached film archive, holding works dating from the 1920s to today and an extensive collection of news reels, is an important resource for students of film and movie professionals. The building is also home to a Holocaust Multimedia Research Center, an institute for education in cinema and media, and a private film library donated by a couple noted for their showbiz philanthropy.

The Cinematheque was founded in 1973 by an Israeli film legend, Lia van Leer (1924–2015), who also established the Israel Film Archive, the Jerusalem Film Festival and the *Haifa Film Centre.*

On the lower floor, the large and cosy Lavan café-restaurant has a long bar and a great view of the Old City. Like the cinema, it opens seven days a week. The restaurant has gained an outstanding reputation with creative, Italian-influenced cuisine. It attracts customers who have no intention of watching a film.

Address 11 Hebron Road, Jerusalem 93546, +972 2 5654333, www.jer-cin.org.il/en | Getting there Bus 7, 8, 18, 34, 38, 71, 72, 74 or 77 to Menachem Begin Heritage Center or Old First Station | Hours Lavan Restaurant: +972 2 6737393, Sun–Thu noon–11pm, Fri & Sat 10am–11pm | Tip The purpose of the Jerusalem House of Quality is to promote art and crafts. Its building with a pleasant courtyard houses a small gallery and a collection of historic artefacts, as well as an Armenian ceramics rooms and a copy of a 2,700-year-old silver roll (12 Hebron Road, +972 2 6717430).

25 The City Wall
The Old City from above

A walk along the city wall shows how astonishingly small the Old City of Jerusalem, which has been fought over for thousands of years, really is. The quarters named after the Christians, Muslims and Jews are just one square kilometre in size. To this can be added the quarter of the Armenian Christians, whose church is one of the very oldest in the Christian world. A much smaller area is that of the Temple Mount, the site of the Western Wall and the neighbouring Church of the Holy Sepulchre, the holy places that are at the heart of the conflicts between the monotheistic religious communities. From the wall, which is up to 20 metres high, you see the many towers, domes, roofs, churches and mosques, but also look down on busy little streets with playing children, washing lines densely hung, satellite dishes and smoking chimneys. The Old City is not just a historical stage set but also a lively place where many people have their homes.

At the Jaffa Gate, you pay admission to start the almost two-kilometre walk along the wall, which was built in the 16th century by Sultan Suleiman the Magnificent on Byzantine and Roman foundations. The Ramparts Tour has two routes with different entry points, both at the Jaffa Gate. One goes north, the other south. You can interrupt the walk at the Damascus Gate, the Lion Gate and the Zion Gate. The parts of the wall right next to the Temple Mount and in the south are not accessible.

The stunning view from the wall across the surroundings of the Old City is the work of the British, who prohibited any new construction here after taking power in 1917. This leaves a view down into the green Hinnom Valley, to the picturesque Montefiore Windmill, the square-looking King David Hotel, the Hebrew University on Mount Zion and the gilded onion domes of the Russian Orthodox Church of St Mary Magdalen on the Mount of Olives.

Address Jaffa Gate, Jerusalem 9114001 | Getting there Tram to City Hall; bus 1, 20 or 38 to Jaffa Gate | Hours Summer, Sun–Thu 9am–5pm, Fri 9am–2pm; winter, Sun–Thu 9am–4pm, Fri 9am–2pm (tickets from the kiosk, on the left next to the steps after passing through the Jaffa Gate) | Tip David's Tower, built by Suleiman the Magnificent as a minaret, stands in David's Citadel in the archaeological park. The tower is home to the municipal museum, containing artefacts and works of art from 4,000 years of history (entrance to the right of the Jaffa Gate, +972 2 6265333, Sat–Thu 9am–4pm, Fri 9am–2pm).

26 Daniel Auster Park

A garden from Ottoman times

The park named after the first Jewish mayor of Jerusalem after Israeli independence, Daniel Auster, a relative of the American writer Paul Auster, is an oasis of peace in the urban bustle. This small green space is flanked by public offices, the old and the new city hall, the tram stop at the end of busy Jaffa Street and by wide Safra Square, where Israeli flags flutter from tall poles. Concerts and other events are held here, while sports fans and supporters of political parties like to celebrate their victories on the square with lots of noise. In summer a piano stands here, and anyone who fancies tinkling the keys can try their hand. Groups of school pupils and soldiers often gather here to sing Israeli songs.

Before 1967 this whole area was on the border between the Israeli western sector and the Jordanian-controlled eastern part of the city. From the massive, circular city hall of West Jerusalem there was a view of the Old City with the Temple Mount and Western Wall – almost inaccessible for Israelis. Since those days, much has been done to smarten up the area. The park, once laid out by Turkish rulers, has thus become the quiet heart of the Jerusalem municipal authorities, who occupy the highly modern buildings as well as the painstakingly restored structures remaining from the Ottoman period.

The charming, European-style garden with well-kept flower beds and palm trees is part of an extensive complex, a little maze of fountains, steps and courtyards. Art installations, modern sculptures, busts and Armenian ceramics embellish the park. Among the most conspicuous works are an outsized blue radio by an Israeli artist and *Modern Head*, a sculpture that the American pop artist Roy Lichtenstein donated in memory of assassinated prime minister Yitzhak Rabin. The city authorities offer tours of the park and Safra Square on Mondays (available in English).

Address Jaffa Road/Safra Square, Jerusalem 9414109 | Getting there Tram to City
Hall | Tip The Putin Bar opposite Safra Square has originality and is very popular, not
only among the many Russians-in-exile. Several kinds of beer on draught, eight kinds
of vodka and Russian specialities are served (19 Jaffa Road, +972 2 528954541).

27 __Dar Al-Tifel Museum

Political messages behind costumes

The flow of visitors to this museum is not overwhelming. On the one hand, the attractive mansion with a large courtyard dating from late Ottoman times that houses it is in East Jerusalem, off the beaten tourist track. On the other hand, the Palestinian Heritage Museum is not blessed with spectacular artefacts. However, the modern, extremely well-kept building exhibits many fine and impressive items from Palestinian history, including traditional costumes and everyday clothing, jewellery, ceramics, furniture, carpets, weapons, tools, documents and books. Only when you look more closely does it become clear that the museum, situated near the luxurious American Colony Hotel, is also a highly political institution that tells of the fate of the Palestinians.

The woman who founded the museum, Hind Taher Al-Husseini, a teacher and social worker, saved many children who had lost their families following an alleged massacre carried out by Israeli underground fighters in the village of Deir Yasin in 1948. Israeli historians say that there were many civilian casualties in the bitter battle because Arab fighters had taken up positions in the residents' homes. A Palestinian film about the disputed events in Deir Yasin is shown in the museum. There is a scale model of the village and a map of Palestine showing 450 Arab settlements that were destroyed during the Israeli War of Independence, which the Palestinians call the 'nakba' (catastrophe).

In 1948, Hind Taher Al-Husseini set up an orphanage in her grandfather's villa. This eventually became a large institute, with further schools and kindergartens at a different location in Jerusalem. On her initiative, in 1978 the family house was converted into a museum for the preservation of Palestinian culture, then known as the 'Museum Al-Tifl Al-Arabi' (The Home of the Arab Child), and later given its present name.

Address Abu Obaidah Al-Jarrah Street, East Jerusalem 9795506, +972 2 6272531, www.dta-museum.org/en | Getting there Bus 17 to Derekh Shem / Louis Vincent | Hours Mon–Wed, & Sat 9am–3pm, Thu 9am–6pm | Tip Of the imposing tomb of Queen Helena of Adiabene (Mesopotamia), dating from about 50 CE, only ruins remain, with 7 burial chambers and 48 funeral niches. The tomb of the queen, who converted to Judaism, was discovered in 1895 and at first was thought to have been a tomb of kings of Judaea (Saladin Street, Mon–Sat 8am–12.30pm & 2–5pm).

28__The Design District

Young fashion and jewellery designers

The boutiques are often tiny, the jewellers' shops hidden away, the galleries inconspicuous, and guests at the street café only discover its home-made delicacies if they know which corner of the place they have to seek out. In the maze of buildings between Ben Yehuda Street and King George Street, off the tourist trail, many a secret place for shopping can be found.

There is still a sign saying 'Design District' at the corner of Ben Yehuda Street and Bezalel Street. It was placed there when the city authorities wanted to establish a centre for young creators of fashion, designers and craft producers between the high-class residential area of Nahlaot and the main shopping district. The idea behind this initiative was to help Jerusalem to remain attractive for non-religious citizens. For decades, in view of the high birth rate of the strictly pious Jews and the immigration of the orthodox, the city has become increasingly dominated by religious citizens, thus reinforcing the exodus of young people to the vibrant beach city of Tel Aviv with its flourishing economy and its enormous range of leisure activities.

The designer zone was intended to attract fashion and jewellery designers, goldsmiths, glass artists, engravers, carvers and potters with low rents for workshops and stores. The project was successful, but when municipal funding came to an end, many of the businesses had to close. The ones with staying power appealed to customers through creativity and quality. Anat Friedmann, for example, whose boutique of the same name sells only her own designs, classic dresses, skirts and blouses. The shoemaker Adi Kilav creates handbags as well as hand-made shoes. The shop Sofia ventures to offer avant-garde fashion and accessories by both renowned and unknown designers. Many of the latter are graduates of the Bezalel Academy, the national university of the arts.

Address Kedem Sasson, 21 King George Street, Anat Friedman, 6 Bezalel Street, Sofia, 2 Bezalel Street, Jerusalem 9426104 | Getting there Bus 1, 7 or 19 to Bezalel/Trumpeldor | Tip Café Bezalel is a small eatery for students and artists. On the menu are lots of home-made cakes and other pastries, various options for breakfast and light meals, some of them vegetarian and vegan (open on the Shabbat, 8 Bezalel Street).

29 ___ The 'Ecce Homo' Arch
Myths in the Convent of the Sisters of Zion

Dramatic stories surround the Roman arch in the Via Dolorosa. Some historians think that violent clashes between the Romans and Jewish rebels took place on this very spot in the year 70 CE. Some archaeologists believe that the arch was part of the east gate of Jerusalem. Others regard it as the entrance to the Antonia Fortress, a Roman legionary fortification. According to a legend, the arch marks the spot where the Roman governor Pontius Pilate – as described in St John's Gospel – presented Jesus Christ to the people with the words 'Ecce homo' ('Behold the man' in Latin) before sentencing him to death.

In 135 CE, following the defeat of the Jewish rebels led by Bar Kochba, the Roman emperor Hadrian rebuilt the city, which had been almost completely destroyed. Hadrian called it 'Aelia Capitolana' – and this was to be the name of Jerusalem for centuries. He used the remains of the gate to build a triumphal arch in the middle of the forum.

All that can be seen in the Via Dolorosa today, at the second of the 14 stations marking the passion of Christ, is the central part of the 3 arches of the gateway. In the construction of the Convent of the Sisters of Zion in the mid-19th century, the northern part of the arch was integrated into the convent church, the Ecce Homo Basilica, where it stands directly behind the altar. The large and impressive crypt of the church has been restored with some cost and effort. Many finds from excavations, some of them from antiquity, can be seen here, and in a further room there is a cistern, now covered by the street above. The southern arch of the gateway has largely been destroyed and is situated in the Ezbekiyeh Dervish monastery. The west side of the arch bears an inscription, no longer complete, in Greek. This may be a passage from St Luke's Gospel, with the words 'Take him away, crucify him!'

Address 41 Via Dolorosa, Jerusalem 9762641, +972 2 6277292 (basilica) | **Getting there** The quickest route is from the Damascus Gate, along El Wad Street, then left to the Via Dolorosa | **Hours** Basilica Mon–Fri 9am–noon & 2–5pm, Sat 9am–5pm (fully accessible only for guests of the pilgrim hostel Ecce Homo Convent; www.eccehomopilgrimhouse.com) | **Tip** The Armenian Catholic church, the Church of Our Lady of Sorrows, is station no. four on the Via Dolorosa. In the crypt, in the architectural style of the Crusader period, is a floor mosaic of the 4th to 6th century (36 Via Dolorosa).

30__The Ein Yael Museum

Hands-on ancient history

Jerusalem is child-friendly, as is the whole of Israel. One of the most exciting places for children and young people is the Ein Yael Living Museum. Beautifully situated in the green Emek Refaim valley, on the outskirts of the city, this visitor experience among ancient sites invites everyone to join in. There are workshops and courses for basket-making, textile-weaving and music, for pottery, painting and creating mosaics. Children can also get involved in threshing wheat, milking cows, baking pitta bread and cooking food on a camp fire. In the right season, they can even produce oil from an olive press or turn grapes into juice.

The techniques and activities are usually ones that were important in ancient times. In the idyllic environment of Ein Yael (which means 'spring of the mountain goat'), since 1998 children have been familiarised through playful means with both agriculture and history at one and the same time. However, in this theme park with its variety of experiences it is also possible just to wander around and look at everything.

The 40-hectare area on the edge of the city was integrated into an archaeological site discovered in 1977, which has ancient terraces, an old irrigation system, a well and the ruins of a Roman villa with a bathhouse and beautiful restored frescoes and mosaics. The museum project, which is funded by the Jerusalem Foundation, also includes orchards and small wheatfields, as well as a reconstructed Roman road with little shops and workshops.

The project runs not only courses, day excursions and summer camps but also programmes for children with handicaps, for young people with problems and new immigrants. In pottery workshops, Jewish and Arab children are acquainted with their shared heritage of craft work. The museum is especially lively when actors and musicians take their audience on a playful trip into ancient times.

Address Malha, Jerusalem 91481, +972 2 6451866, www.projects.jerusalemfoundation.org, office@einyael.co.il | Getting there Bus 26a or 33 to Malha | Hours Sun–Thu 10am–4pm, courses by advance booking, by arrangement for groups | Tip The nearby Biblical Zoo presents animals mentioned in the Bible, but also other species that are endangered (1 Derech Aharon Shulov, +972 2 6750111, Sun–Thu 9am–5pm, 6pm in summer, Fri 9am–4.30pm, Sat 10am–5pm).

31_ The Einstein Monument

A symbol for a city of science

Albert Einstein would surely have liked the spot where his monument stands in the Hebrew University. He was a great supporter of the university, and the two and a half-metre-high bronze statue was placed in the park of the Edmond J. Safra Campus, close to the institutes of mathematics and physics and to the imposing national library. Fittingly for a brilliant natural scientist, he does not gaze meditatively into the distance but seems to look at the beholder in front of him in a down-to-earth, friendly but critical way.

In 2015, to mark the 100th anniversary of the theory of relativity and the 60th anniversary of his death, the statue by the Russian sculptor Georgy Frangulyan was unveiled. It is surprising that this happened so late – after all, the history of this world-famous university, which laid the foundations for Jerusalem as a place of science with its many institutes and academies, was always closely connected with Einstein. To this day, the university benefits from income from the works and patents of the Nobel Prize winner, and the bequest of his writings is here, in accordance with his will.

Einstein always supported the idea of a Jewish state in Palestine, even though he never joined a Zionist organisation, and in 1952 declined to become president of Israel. As a young man, he even left the Jewish religious community. In the face of the heated anti-Semitic mood in the Weimar Republic, however, in 1924 he became a member of the Jewish congregation in Berlin – out of solidarity with Judaism, not because he had become religious. The university in Jerusalem was extremely close to Einstein's heart, and he collected donations for it in the USA. In 1923, he attended the founding ceremony, and in 1925 became a member of the university council. Until his death, he supported the institution academically and financially, and included it in his will.

Address Edmond J. Safra Campus, Givat Ram, Jerusalem 39105 | **Getting there** Bus 7, 7h, 9, 14, 35, 35h, 42, 66, 66h or 68 to Hebrew University | **Tip** The National Library of Israel is an architecturally exciting building that possesses several Einstein documents and the first publication on the theory of relativity. There is an exhibition of ancient maps, and the design of the windows is beautiful (Sun–Thu 9am–8pm, Fri 9am–1pm, visitor centre Sun–Thu 9am–3pm).

32___Elia's Photo Shop
A treasure trove for old pictures of Jerusalem

The eventful history of Jerusalem since the end of the 19th century comes alive in this little shop, painted gaudy yellow outside. Some of its many thousand photographs in black-and-white or sepia were taken in the age of Ottoman rule. They reflect fashions long ago, but also everyday life in the Holy City, which has never become a melting pot but was usually torn between different religions, peoples and groups.

The proprietor Kevork Kahvedjian and his son are continuing the tradition of Kevork's legendary father, the Armenian photographer Elia Kahvedjian (1910–1999), whose photographic treasures, most of them taken with an analogue Rolleiflex camera, are still freshly developed in an old-fashioned darkroom. Photos of Jerusalem on which mules, donkeys and horse-drawn carts characterise the street scene, and rare shots of the Six-Day War attract diplomats and lovers of historic images from all over the world to this shop.

Armenians brought photography to the Middle East in the second half of the 19th century. On the initiative of the Armenian patriarch at that time, Yesai Garabedian, workshops on photography were held in Jerusalem for the first time – even leading some young priests to change their profession.

In 1915, Elia Kahvedjian, a five-year-old orphan who had lost his family in the genocide committed on the Armenians, came to Nazareth by indirect ways with other Armenian children. As a young man, he gained a reputation as a photographer, and his shop in the Christian Quarter of Jerusalem became a place where locals of all religions came for portraits and passport photos, or for photos for their family and wedding albums. At the same time, he became an important chronicler of this frequently fought-over city with its changing rulers. His unique photos of Jerusalem are shown in exhibitions across the world to this day.

Address 14 Al Khanka Street, Jerusalem 9531220, +972 2 6282074, www.eliaphoto.com | Getting there From the Jaffa Gate or the New Gate to the Christian Quarter of the Old City; the shop is near the Church of the Holy Sepulchre | Hours Irregular, usually Mon–Sat 10am–5pm, often closed for a short time at midday | Tip The relatively new Terra Sancta Museum is devoted to the roots of Christianity and the history of the Via Dolorosa. The exhibition presents important archaeological finds from the age of Herod to the present (1 Via Dolorosa, summer daily 9am–6pm, winter daily 9am–5pm).

33__ The Elvis Monument

A stopover for the king of rock

The Neve Ilan highway service station near the Israeli-Arab town of Abu Gosh has been a place of pilgrimage for Elvis fans in the Holy Land for decades. Pop stars including Joe Cocker, Sting and Michael Jackson have also paid visits to this remarkable cult site in the Judaean hills during their tours of Israel.

Uri Yoeli, an Israeli and a passionate admirer of the legendary American rock singer since his childhood, bought the land with a petrol station, a guest house and a few small shops on a rocky hillside in 1974. Since then a bronze statue of the singing superstar, shining gold and five metres tall, has stood in front of the Elvis Inn restaurant. From this spot, visitors have a wonderful view across to the Trappist monastery of Latrun and over the broad valley to the coastal plain of Tel Aviv.

In the classic diner-style restaurant with lots of chrome, plastic and red colours, hundreds of Elvis photos, posters and albums cover the walls. Countless items of Elvis memorabilia – mugs, glasses, ashtrays, bottles of wine and magnets with Elvis motifs – are on sale, as well as T-shirts bearing the claim 'I saw Elvis at…', with pictures of the rock-'n'-roll star at the Western Wall or on the beach at Tel Aviv. Life-size bronze Elvis figures sit at the tables and stand casually at the long bar. It goes without saying that his voice croons and rocks ceaselessly from the juke-box. Diner classics such as hamburgers and hotdogs feature on the menu – though local specialities like hummus, tahini and shawarma, too, are essential here.

Each year on 8 January a crowd of fans of the king of rock assembles at Neve Ilan to celebrate his birthday. On the anniversary of his death, too, 16 August, there are parties, sometimes wild, with Elvis impersonators, girls in petticoats and boys in tight jeans whose hot heels glide over the dance floor in 1960s' style.

Address **Elvis Inn Neve Ilan, Abu Gosh, Jerusalem 9085000, +972 2 5341275** | Getting there Bus 185 to Neve Ilan A and B; national route 1 towards Tel Aviv, exit for Abu Gosh | Hours Restaurant: daily 7am–7pm (liable to changes) | Tip The Church of the Resurrection in Abu Gosh, a fortress-like Romanesque Crusader church built in the 12th century, has beautiful frescoes and outer walls up to 3.7 metres thick. It is part of the Benedictine monastery in the centre of the small town.

34 Eucalyptus

Biblical meals on the menu

The nicest possible place to sit is at a table on the terrace beneath the eucalyptus tree at the heart of the small artists' quarter, a stone's throw from the old city wall. This restaurant in a restored 19th-century building is remarkable in many ways: head chef Moshe Basson prepares meals with biblical connections. The three tasting menus are named after King David, the Queen of Sheba and the Song of Songs, the love poem from the Bible. The red lentil stew is nicknamed 'The Jacob and Esau Special', a reference to Jacob, who bought Esau's birthright in return for a lentil dish.

Basson, who, incidentally, greets all his diners personally, believes that his cooking existed in this or a similar form 2,000 years ago. His specialities include figs stuffed with chicken meat in tamarind sauce, fried aubergines with tahini and pomegranate syrup, wild duck with pear, and couscous dishes. The ma'aluba ceremony is a minor spectacle in the restaurant. This traditional stew with meat on a bed of rice and vegetables is simmered for many hours and then up-ended at the table straight from the casserole on to the diner's plate. As this happens, a fanfare sounds and the waiters beat copper bowls and pan lids with cooking spoons.

Basson, who had to flee from Iraq in the 1960s, is proud of his successful and spacious restaurant in the upper price bracket. He has won several gourmet awards, and has experimented a lot so that he can present his modern interpretation of biblical cuisine. His acclaimed restaurant is affiliated to the high-class international Slow Food movement, and attaches great importance to fresh, regional ingredients. Many of the herbs come from Basson's own garden. Each meal starts with simple, delicious, home-baked bread that comes straight from the oven and three spreads, made from tahini, dried tomatoes in olive oil and aubergine with walnuts.

Address 14 Hativat Yerushalayim Street, Hutzot HaYotzer Colony, Jerusalem 9411700, +972 2 6244331, www.the-eucalyptus.com | Getting there Bus 38, 83, 124, 125 or 163 to the Jaffa Gate | Hours Sun–Thu 5–11pm, Sat 8.15–11pm | Tip The wide pedestrian path where Eucalyptus is located is the Hutzot Hayotzer artists' colony, with 26 studios and art galleries, built in 1969. Here an annual craft festival and occasional concerts are held. There are also small markets and exhibitions, and many artists open their studios to visitors (Sun–Thu 10am–5pm, Fri 10am–2pm).

35__The Express Station
Off to Tel Aviv from 80 metres below the ground

High-tech in the Holy City: the futuristic-looking building that houses the new Yitzhak Nawon Station sends the message that, after a 17-year construction period for the project for an express train to Tel Aviv, expectations are high. The aim is above all to shift road traffic on to the rail tracks: the trains, running every 15 minutes, could transport up to 1,000 people. The 35 lifts would take passengers to an underground shopping and office level and to the four platforms of the subterranean station, which was also conceived as a shelter for 2,000 people.

Although Israel's two most important cities are only 65 kilometres apart, a journey by car or bus used to take an hour, and the old rail service was even slower. The new trains, which will set off from north-west Jerusalem 80 metres below the ground, take only 28 minutes despite making a stop at Ben Gurion Airport – and will benefit from the absence of traffic jams. The 60-kilometre rail link with many bridges and tunnels (up to 11 kilometres long) is Israel's first fully electrified line. The red double-decker carriages, a model called Twindexx Vario, made in Germany, will move at a top speed of 160 kilometres per hour. The government wants to extend the route to the Old City of Jerusalem. Then it would be possible to travel directly from the beach in Tel Aviv to the Western Wall in Jerusalem in half an hour.

The consequences of this new connection for Israel are not clear. The government hopes this will make Jerusalem more attractive for business. Employees who prefer to live in Tel Aviv, a city of pleasure that has a beach, will be able to commute more easily. Pessimists fear that even more non-religious citizens of Jerusalem than before will move to the coast and only come to Jerusalem in the daytime to their places of work in ministries, public offices and institutions.

Address Yitzchak Nawon, between Shedrot Shazar Boulevard and Jaffa Road, Jerusalem 9411714 | **Getting there** Bus 3, 6, 14, 31, 32, 50, 54, 66, 67, 68, 74, 75 or 78 to Central Station | **Tip** The neighbouring old Jerusalem station, Malcha, was the most important in the city for a long time. It was the terminus of the Tel Aviv/ Jaffa–Jerusalem route. The new link means its future is uncertain.

36 — The Falafel Temple

Abu Shukri – the controversial falafel king

The question of the best falafel in Jerusalem is as controversial as that of the best hot dog in New York or the best fish and chips in London. Jerusalem citizens get emotionally involved when they discuss where the city's most popular kind of warm fast food tastes best. For years now, many residents of the Holy City have voted Abu Shukri their 'falafel king'. There are indeed good arguments for this old-established restaurant near the Via Dolorosa, which is run today by the grandchildren of Shukri, the famous, long-dead 'father' ('Abu' in Arabic) who founded it.

For one thing, the eatery, which has existed for 70 years, is visibly successful. The soberly furnished room with seating for about two dozen people is always full of people, not only in the tourist season.

Secondly, there are professed adherents of Abu Shukri in all three of the major religious communities – something not to be taken for granted in Jerusalem, especially in relation to this dish. In contrast to other falafel specialists, Abu Shukri keeps its heavy cauldrons of oil, in which the chickpea balls made on the premises are deep-fried, in the kitchen at the back, instead of at the entrance. This is a sign that the restaurant can rely on its good reputation: it is not necessary to convince strolling passers-by that everything is home-made here.

Enthusiasm for falafel and equally for hummus, a chickpea purée, creates culinary unity among religious and ethnic groups that otherwise disagree. The recipes for various specialities made from chickpeas do not differ in essentials. Boiled until soft, these pulses, which were already eaten in Asia Minor 8,000 years ago according to archaeologists, are mixed with olive oil, herbs, spices, baking powder, sesame, bulgur wheat, garlic, onions and lemon (according to taste), then served with warm pitta bread.

Address El Wad Street 63, Jerusalem 9710700, +972 2 6271538; Hummus Lina, Ma'a lot E-Chanka Street 42, Jerusalem 17392, +972 2 6277230 | Getting there Tram to the Damascus Gate, from there follow El Wad Street to the Old City | Hours Daily 8am–4.30pm | Tip Abu Shukri has many respected competitors, for example Hummus Lina in the Christian Quarter (Al Khanka Street) and the restaurant Waari, a few hundred metres from the Damascus Gate in Salah ed Din Street.

37 The Festival Hall

A symbol of reconciliation between religions

In Jerusalem, there are few institutions that devote themselves to bringing together people of all religions. One of these is the concert hall in the impressive YMCA complex, which puts on a packed programme of concerts and other performances. Even the architecture and fittings of the Golden Hall of Friendship symbolically express an inter-religious message of tolerance and reconciliation. The 12 windows of the domed hall represent the 12 tribes of Israel and the 12 followers of Mohammed. The cross, crescent moon and star of David are depicted on the splendid chandeliers and the brass lamps on the side walls.

The Jerusalem base of the Young Men's Christian Association, opened in 1933, set itself the aim from the beginning of promoting peaceful coexistence among the greatly divided population of the Holy City. On the façade, quotes from the Bible in Hebrew, English and Arabic call for unity and peace. The architect of this 'place of peace' with its idyllic gardens and the city's oldest indoor swimming pool was an American, Arthur L. Harmon, who designed the Empire State Building in New York. The almost 50-metre-high tower of the Three Arches Hotel in the YMCA complex, which also contains a cinema and a small archaeological museum, is one of the city's most striking landmarks.

For more than 20 years its 600-seat concert hall has been a venue for the prestigious annual Jerusalem International Chamber Music Festival. The founder and artistic director of the festival, the Russian pianist Elena Bashkirova, often succeeds in attracting excellent, world-renowned musicians, who play without taking a fee in this fascinating, magical place. These stars have included the violinists Madeleine Carruzzo and Gidon Kremer, the cellist Julian Steckel, the flautist Emmanuel Pahud and of course the conductor Daniel Barenboim, Bashkirova's husband.

هذا مكان بسوده السلام هبته بمكان
نسيان الأغفار السياسية والدينية ومن تتابع
الوحدة العالمية ان نحو وتزدهر
من خطبة الاميركي اللهي قد عبد الورود الثاني في نيسان ١٩٣٢

HERE IS A PLACE WHOSE
ATMOSPHERE IS PEACE
WHERE POLITICAL AND RELIGIOUS
JEALOUSIES CAN BE FORGOTTEN
AND INTERNATIONAL UNITY BE
FOSTERED AND DEVELOPED

מקום זה – השלום שורר בו
יריבות מדינית ודתית תישכח
אחדות בין עמים תטופח ותתפתח
קטע מנאום ההקדשה של לורד אלנבי – אפריל גני

Address 26 King David Street, Jerusalem 91002, +972 2 5692694, www.ymca.org.il | Getting there Bus 4, 7, 8, 13, 18, 21, 30a, 38, 49, 71, 72, 74, 75, 101, 102, 103, 105, 106, 107 or 108 to David HaMelekh/Mapu or Yemin Moshe | Tip The viewing platform on the bell tower of the YMCA has a stunning view of Jerusalem. Non-residents of the hotel can take the lift to the top for a small fee (€1.25) – ask at the reception.

38_ The First Backpacker

A hostel for learning, joining in and enjoyment

Although the managers of the hostel stress that guests from all age groups love their accommodation, young people are of course the dominant group at this colourfully furnished, spacious guesthouse, which advertises its services with the slogan 'the first backpacker'. It is run like a perfectly normal hotel with many double rooms, and provides much more than merely its 300 beds, a breakfast room and some quirky graffiti on the walls. It also has a remarkably lovely roof terrace, large rooms for meetings and workshops, and an unusual events programme.

On Sundays the Abraham Hostel, which is centrally located in the city centre, holds an open jam session, when the bands and singers who perform their music are usually young. Sometimes guests are allowed to take the stage and join in, and after this anyone who wants can show their skills at the piano or play the instrument that they have brought along – solo or together. Many guests at the hostel take a guitar, violin, oboe or drum with them on their travels.

In the large common room on the first floor are settees and arm-chairs, hammocks and beanbags, tables and chairs, a pool table and table football. There is plenty of space for anyone who wants to dance. Alternatively, you can sit at the counter of the professionally run bar with a glass of draught beer or fresh fruit juice, or enjoy a snack. On some evenings there is a pub quiz or a film screening, even a pub crawl, and dinner is eaten collectively on the eve of Shabbat – though this is only for hostel residents. In summer, there is a barbecue on the roof once a week. During the day, hostel guests can take part in yoga workshops or learn the right way to prepare hummus. At the 'language exchange' events, people who have come to the hostel from countries all over the world converse together playfully and joyfully in their various languages.

Address 67 Hanevi'm Street, Jerusalem 9470211, +972 2 3932793, www.abrahamhostels.com/jerusalem | Getting there Tram, bus 7, 25, 32, 66, 75 or 77 to HaDavidka | Tip The Hamotzi Restaurant near the Mahane Yehuda Market has a show kitchen, and in summer diners can sit at tables on the pavement in this lively spot. All dishes are freshly prepared. On the menu are meats from the grill and Israeli-European cuisine that has won multiple awards (113 Jaffa Street, +972 2 6310050, Sun–Thu noon–midnight, Fri 11.30am–3pm).

39__First Station

Art, music and pubs in the old station

First Station is not typical of Jerusalem – above all because there are considerable cultural, culinary and sporting activities in this carefully restored and altered old station dating from 1892, even on the Shabbat. Usually Jerusalem – apart from the Arab eastern part – seems unnaturally quiet on the Jewish holy day. Municipal buses and the tram do not run, and other forms of traffic are largely at rest too. The city scene is dominated by orthodox families, often in traditional festive clothing, on their way to the synagogue and by children playing in generally empty streets.

On Friday evening, First Station therefore becomes a place of refuge for a good 24 hours for Israelis less committed to their faith and for tourists. But there is something on offer for religious citizens and visitors to the city: on Friday before sunset the musical Kabbalat Shabbat is performed on the central stage, and on Saturday evening the ritual conclusion of Shabbat, the so-called havdalah service, is celebrated.

On seven days in the week, restaurants, bars, galleries, market stalls and shops, as well as concerts that are usually free, theatre performances, and other events draw the public to First Station at the edge of the German Colony. Only a few of the shops close on Saturdays. The well-kept leisure park, shaded in places with artistically painted sails, where bikes and Segways can be hired, is especially family-friendly. In a large tent at the edge of the arts centre there is a play area for small children, that includes wall climbing and inflatable jumping facilities. Here they can also work off energy without danger on the car-free grounds of First Station.

The culinary offerings range from beer gardens, falafel stalls and ice cream parlours to remarkable restaurants such as Beit Hakavan, Station 9 and Adom, which is part of a renowned chain of speciality restaurants.

Address 4 David Remez Street, Jerusalem 9354102, +972 72 3290728, www.firststation.co.il/en | **Getting there** Bus 71, 72 or 74 to Hahan / David Remez | **Hours** Daily 7am – midnight, though not all shops, stalls and restaurants | **Tip** The Matthäus Frank House, one of the oldest and most impressive buildings in the German Colony, was constructed in 1873 by the Templer Matthäus Frank, who intended to found a Templer community in this way (6 Emek Refaim Street).

40_ The Gatsby Room
A bar with an educational mission

'Immerse yourself in another world' is the promise at this bar in Jerusalem, which specialises in cocktails. This already starts at the entrance, which is not easy to find in a large corner building, and confusingly only leads to a small room with a reception desk and wardrobe. However, a wallpapered door disguised as a bookcase then slides open – in the spirit of the Prohibition era in the USA, where illegal speakeasies were to be found hidden behind all kinds of frontages.

With its metal-clad ceiling, stylish Art Deco lights and mirrors, and classic bar stools, the interior is an accomplished act of homage to the Roaring Twenties, as captured by Scott Fitzgerald in *The Great Gatsby*. The background music, too – often swing and jazz – is from the 1920s and 1930s. Sometimes bands give live concerts to match the style of the bar. There is a separate room for smokers.

Behind the bar counter in the elegant lounge experienced and committed bar tenders prepare more than a dozen of their own cocktail creations, as well as the classics, of course. The newly invented drinks include such distinctive cocktails as Crossroad, for which Irish whiskey is mixed with fig jam, agave syrup and lemon, then pepped up with smoked rosemary. Then there is the Fitzgerald – gin, lemon, egg white and bitters. The barman will also mix something according to a theme or a particular alcoholic ingredient if the customer wishes. The snacks are remarkable: ambitious creations from crossover cuisine, with Japanese, Israeli and Peruvian influences. The owners of the Gatsby Room want to establish a cocktail culture in Jerusalem. Indeed, in Israel there is traditionally hardly any culture of drinking. In the first decades of the state's existence, the goals were to survive and build, with lofty ideals and political visions. Not much alcohol was drunk at all – especially in religious Jerusalem.

Address Gatsby Cocktail Room, 18 Hillel Street, Jerusalem 9458118, +972 54 8147143, www.facebook.com/GatsbyJerusalem (entrance at the end of the terrace in front of Café Aroma) | Getting there Tram to Yaffo Center; bus 7, 13, 19, 22 or 77 to King George / Ben Yehuda | Hours Daily 6pm–1am | Tip For two decades, one of the most popular Italian restaurants in Jerusalem has been the Focaccia Bar, just round the corner from Gatsby's. Classic Italian dishes are served here (Rabi Akiva 4, +972 2 6256428, www.bar.focaccia.co).

41_ The Glen Whisky Bar

A pub with its own whisky and beer

Leon Shwartz, the bar owner, loves alcohol, as he explains himself. Because he is particularly keen on whisky, he stocks almost 400 brands from all over the world, two of them from Israel. The lovingly designed drinks menu is dominated by malts from Scotland, including special editions and such rarities as a 37-year-old Port Ellen matured in a Sherry cask. The Glen Whisky Bar has earned an international reputation and gains high praise in bar guidebooks; its good name has led whisky distilleries to give talks and presentations in the bar.

But this small place with a long bar and a wooden gallery also serves, alongside an extensive assortment of spirits from all over the world, 20 kinds of draught beer. Among them are nine craft beers from Israel alone, as well as products from the Czech Republic, Germany and England. The house specialities are its own beer, to which whisky and honey are added before it is matured in oak barrels, and a kind of mead with ginger. For hungry customers, there are burgers and shepherd's pie, pasta and snacks.

On Wednesdays, bands or solo musicians perform live, with a programme ranging from rock and blues to jazz and folk music. Festivals are celebrated as they come round: on Tartan Day and St Patrick's Day beer and whisky from Scotland and Ireland are on offer, and some guests come in matching costume, wearing a tartan kilt or clad from head to foot in Irish emerald green.

Unusually for Jerusalem, this bar opens seven days a week, and often does not close until four or five o'clock in the morning. Shwartz cultivates a casual atmosphere. There is no dress code, and great importance is attached to tolerance. This is one reason why the bar is popular with some exotic characters. As far as music is concerned, it is obvious that the professional bar keepers, Tom Castel and Shmuel Naky, like classic rock and blues.

Address 18 Queen Shlomtzion Street, Jerusalem 9414614, +972 54 901007, www.facebook.com/glen.w.bar | Getting there Bus 13, 19, 104, 105, 108, 115, 284, 480 or 755 to Mamilla/Agron Street | Hours Daily 7pm–4am | Tip The two-storey Café Caffit, diagonally opposite in a small pedestrian zone with tables outside, is a rendezvous for Jerusalem celebrities. Home-made pasta, various kinds of pizza and flatbreads are served (36 Emek Refa'im Street, Sun–Thu 7.30am–1am, Fri 7.30am–8pm, Sat 6.30pm–1am, +972 2 5635284).

42 The Gush Katif Museum
A house of radical Zionists

There are Israelis who dream of a Greater Israel. Some orthodox Jews and settlers do not believe in peaceful coexistence with Palestinians and neighbouring Arab states, aiming instead to create an 'Eretz Israel' (a complete land of Israel), extending into Lebanon and other areas. A place that reflects the philosophy and arguments of the radicals is the Gush Katif Museum, which is run by a radical Zionist organisation.

The subject of the exhibition is the fate of the 8,000 Jewish settlers of Gush Katif, who lost their homes in the Gaza Strip in 2005. After Prime Minister Ariel Sharon enforced Israeli withdrawal from the Gaza Strip, the army applied force against angry settlers. This issue divided Israeli society at the time across political parties.

The exhibition, which includes Torah scrolls, pictures and artefacts, documents the events when the residents of 21 Jewish settlements were forced to leave the Gaza Strip within 48 hours. This ended the Israeli presence in Gaza after a period of 38 years. The Palestinians enthusiastically celebrated the withdrawal. The museum highlights the dramatic consequences of the retreat: in conflicts between Palestinian organisations, hundreds of people died in the Gaza Strip in the space of weeks, and the abandoned synagogues were torched. The number of rockets launched at Israel and attacks on Israelis increased. For radical Zionists, these developments are the proof that every withdrawal is interpreted as a sign of weakness rather than a step on the road to a peaceful solution.

The museum also shows that, historically, Gaza also has a Jewish past, dating back to the time of King Solomon. The museum emphasises that it has no political orientation, while presenting in its multimedia displays and works of art a highly one-sided view of the matter, but also one important aspect of the dispute about the path to peace.

Address 5 Sha'arei Tsedek Street, Jerusalem 9436011, +972 2 6255456, http://en.gushkatifmuseum.com | Getting there Tram to Mahane Yehuda; bus 8, 18, 25, 32, 74, 77 or 78 to Shukanyon Agripas | Hours Sun–Thu 10am–6pm, Fri 10am–2pm (shorter hours during winter months) | Tip The BeerBazaar at the Mahane Yehuda Market is a popular spot. This little pub stocks 100 different kinds of craft beer, especially from Israeli micro-breweries, and also produces two kinds of its own (3 Rehov Ets Khayim, Mahane Yehuda Market, +972 2 6712559, Sun–Wed 11–2am, Thu 11–3am, Fri 9.30am–5pm, Sat 8.30pm–2am).

43__G. W. Bush Plaza
A shy message in light by the roadside

Few monuments are as modest as the small square opposite the Mamilla Mall that honours George W. Bush, the former president of the United States. On the other hand, not many monuments include a tree, illuminated at night with twinkling lights like a Christmas tree. Another reason why George W. Bush Plaza is special is that very few memorials at all have been dedicated to this US president (2001 – 2009), who enjoyed little international popularity, and who started the second Iraq War with dubious justification and conducted it without much success.

The small square in a corner, with pale Jerusalem stone, a few trees and three benches, is a well-liked spot for those seeking some shade, as well as peace and quiet on a busy street. A small commemorative stone records the state visit in 2008 of the Republican president, a 'loyal partner to the state of Israel', as the inscription states.

The plaza was paid for by the private New Jerusalem Foundation, which continues to take care of it. It is not funded by the Israeli state. One explanation for this may be that relations between Israel and the Bush government were not without tension. Shortly before Bush visited Jerusalem, an important square in the city was officially named after Jonathan Pollard, who was imprisoned in the USA for espionage. Despite all pleas by the Israeli government in Jerusalem, Bush refused to pardon Pollard, an Israeli citizen.

The background to this inconspicuous memorial casts light on the special relationship between Israel and the USA, traditionally the most important and loyal ally of the Jewish state. President Donald Trump became a hero for many Israelis by transferring the seat of the American embassy from Tel Aviv to Jerusalem in 2018. 'Trump, you have made Israel great again': this message, written in English on large banners, stood for months on various buildings in Jerusalem.

Address George W. Bush Plaza, on King David Street/Agron Street, Jerusalem 9418118 | Getting there Tram to City Hall | Tip The gourmet restaurant 1868 is famed for its innovative cuisine and unusual combinations such as duck with various fruits or veal sweetbread with onion confit. It occupies an old stone-built house and has a beautiful little garden (10 King David Street, +972 2 6222312, www.1868.co.il).

44 __ HaMazkeka
Cross-genre art and liquor

In his ambitious non-profit project, Mikael Berkowitsch is looking for a connection between art and alcoholic spirits – both of which are clearly close to his heart. 'HaMazkeka' means 'The Distillery', and refers to the aim of its initiator to distil his own spirits, which will be served at HaMazkeka. However, the focus of this non-commercial venue, hidden behind the main post office and a little out of the way, is on 'contemporary and interdisciplinary art'.

Since 2014 it has served as a stage for innovative, usually young musicians, filmmakers, media artists and theatre people. HaMazkeka is meant to be a 'space for experiment and creation' – but those who go there find themselves first of all in an extremely lively club with loud music, often with dozens of guests standing and drinking outside the wide-open door.

Nevertheless, the project also has serious and ambitious aims. It not only gives a public stage to artists, but also offers opportunities for artistic production and collaboration thanks to a small but professional recording studio and a workshop space. Berkowitsch, who is of German origin, wishes to find and support artists who are 'up-and-coming and underrated'. Moreover, he wants established artists to have a place where they can try out new forms and paths, creatively and across genres, either alone or with others. HaMazkeka aims to be something like a laboratory for art. Although a wide variety of artists work and perform here, the music – everything from rock and blues to rap, techno, jazz, Balkan, hip-hop and electronic – is often at the centre of attention. Mikael Berkowitsch, who is a musician himself, took inspiration above all from The Stone in New York's East Village, a famous venue where he was delighted at the experimental music performances. *The Jerusalem Post* described his project as a 'precious little gem' on the city's art scene.

Address 3 Shoshan Street, Jerusalem 9414303, +972 2 5822090, www.mazkeka.com | Getting there Tram to City Hall; bus 1, 17, 18, 38, 83a to Kikar Safra | Hours Mon–Sat 7pm–3am | Tip The old city hall with Bauhaus elements, which is still used by the city government, is at the end of Yaffo Street opposite the Old City. In was built in 1930 by the British. The bullet holes in the façade indicate that it was on the border until 1967 (Safra Square).

45__Hamiffal

Alternative projects and way-out art

The somewhat weathered building in the historic Ma'aravim quarter seems, as you enter, like a huge, somewhat anarchic house, imaginatively adorned with posters, sculptures and paintings, run by a commune of musicians, actors, painters, writers, sculptors and craftspeople. At the heart of the large, high-ceilinged rooms, furnished in unorthodox style with old settees and other items that have seen better days, is a tastefully fitted-out café-restaurant – with a small bar and a large choice of vegetarian dishes on the menu.

Hamiffal is the sixth and biggest project of a private initiative called Empty Houses, which was founded in 2011. It looks for unused buildings and converts them, often with considerable assistance from the city government, into alternative centres for the arts. In contrast to other projects, Hamiffal – which means, roughly translated, 'the factory' – is not limited in duration.

It is intended that all forms of art should find a home here. The 19th-century building and its large garden are a single big stage, a workshop and a studio at the same time. Dance and drama, performances and talks take place here, and often rock or jazz concerts. For audiences, most of the events are free of charge. Hamiffal is run on the basis that everyone who wants to join in is welcome, and everyone who wants to try out an idea should get the chance. Visitors from abroad can also participate in principle, though there are varying conditions for the different work groups and project teams.

Hamiffal is one of many private and state-run projects that are trying to increase the attractiveness of Jerusalem, especially for young people. The city is increasingly becoming a thriving artistic and cultural centre, aiming to hold its own against its competitor Tel Aviv, which with its white beaches and exciting nightlife is only 65 kilometres away.

Address 3 Hama'aravim Street, Jerusalem 9418419, www.hamiffal.com/english, www.facebook.com/hamiffal | **Getting there** Bus 18 or 38 to Mamila/Agron Street | **Hours** Sun–Thu noon–midnight, Fri noon–4pm, Sat 8pm–midnight | **Tip** The Waldorf Astoria Hotel, expensively restored in 2014, occupies the over 100-year-old building that once housed the legendary and luxurious Palace Hotel. The three-storey building with its curved façade has elements of Roman, Moorish and Arab style, but the Art Deco influence (c. 1920) is also obvious (26–28 Gershon Agron Street).

46__Havilio Square
The heart of the pub scene

No single district in Jerusalem is regarded as the nightlife quarter. The nearest thing to this is the cluster of establishments at the Mahane Yehuda Market and around Havilio Square, where there are dozens of cafés, bars, pubs and beer gardens, quiet family restaurants and trendy clubs that have queues of young people waiting outside the door at night.

On the square and in the surrounding alleys, most places have a large outdoor area with tasteful wooden tables and chairs. The atmosphere is lively and good-humoured, especially on warm summer evenings – which means from May to October in Jerusalem. Often young people loudly sing catchy Israeli songs, and guests in the neighbouring pubs join in. Sometimes dense, aromatic vapours waft across, revealing that a lot of joints are smoked here. In the Knesset, there are moves to legalise marijuana, which up to now has only been permitted for some stated medical usages.

The leader of the pack at Havilio is the Gent Kitchen & Bar, which has the most outdoor tables. Inside it is a classic pub with a long bar and a big screen on the wall for sports broadcasts. Opposite is Alma, a high-class family restaurant serving Israeli food, and round the corner the wood-panelled Bell Wood Bar, with the atmosphere of an English pub and a choice between 100 kinds of whisky. The liveliest place is Zoli's Pub on a corner. This is a dependable place for drinking beer, with long tables outside. Thanks to its reasonable prices, this pub is popular with a young crowd. Two roads, both of them pedestrianised, branch off from Havilio Square. In narrow Josef Rivlin Street you find small bars, shisha parlours and clubs, including Berlin and the popular pub Mike's Place. Wide Shimon Ben Shatach Street is home to some classy restaurants such as Sea Dolphin, specialising in fish, and Gabriel for French *haute cuisine*.

Address Havilio Square, Jerusalem 9424005 | Getting there Tram to City Hall | Hours Daily 6pm–1am | Tip In the evenings the Mahane Yehuda Market turns into one huge pub and a rendezvous for young people. After sunset, the food market with its 250 stalls and shops is an entertainment quarter. Some shops clear out their goods in the evening and serve drinks.

47__The Hidden Work

A vision of heaven in Koresh Street

Marie Balian has nothing more to prove. Her ceramic art is displayed in great museums and her work is appreciated across the world. But Jerusalem, of all places, the city that she loves and where she has been living for more than 50 years, has demeaned her work. Anyone can go and see the *corpus delicti*. A brightly coloured mosaic made from 1,000 ceramic tiles adorns the side wall of a building in Koresh Street. There are few passers-by here, as the street is off the beaten track. To her disappointment, the city authorities have hidden Balian's work, which she donated in 2004, in a side street.

Art critics describe the work, measuring four by six metres and entitled *Views of Paradise*, as a masterpiece of ceramic art. Balian worked on it for six months in order to give the citizens of Jerusalem, in her own words, 'a work of beauty, delight and hope'. The idyllic, harmonious panorama is a play on mythical symbols of nature. It depicts date palms and cypresses, meadows of flowers, gazelles, birds, peacocks with opened tails and flying fish above water.

Marie Balian is an Armenian artist who studied at the academy of art in Lyon. In the 1960s she married into a family that has cultivated the traditional art of Armenian painted ceramics for almost 100 years in Jerusalem. The family studio, managed by her son today, is in East Jerusalem. Here the tiles are painted by hand and fired at a temperature of 1,000 degrees Celsius to make the paints durable and weatherproof.

The story of Armenian ceramic art in Jerusalem began in 1918, when the rulers of the British Mandate commissioned the Armenian ceramicist David Ohannessian to restore the tiles of the Dome of the Rock. Several of his pupils came with him. The most beautiful buildings in Jerusalem are adorned by Armenian tiles today: churches, museums, Jewish and Muslim institutions.

Address 14 Koresh Street, Jerusalem 9414417, www.facebook.com/pg/
armenianceramicsbalian | Getting there Tram to City Hall | Tip The Municipal Art
Gallery often shows works by young unknown painters or sculptors and by new immigrants,
and puts on frequently changing exhibitions (17 Jaffa Road, Sun–Thu 9am–4.30pm).

48__ The Hill of Evil Counsel
The seat of occupying forces and the UN

Since the 14th century, one of the hills outside the city walls has been known as the Hill of Evil Counsel. Here, in the magnificent villa belonging to Caiaphas, the Jewish high priest, the decision to crucify Jesus is said to have been taken. There is no evidence to support this legend, but the hill has played a major symbolic role in modern times. The Israeli author Amos Oz even gave the name *The Hill of Evil Counsel* to his novel about the mood in the dramatic period when the state of Israel was founded.

In the 1930s the British high commissioner built himself a luxuriously equipped headquarter on this site. It was popularly known as the 'governor's palace'. From up here there is a wonderful view across Jerusalem and far into the Judaean desert. After the British departure from Palestine, the United Nations Truce Supervision Organization (UNTSO), which was formed in 1948 in response to the war on Israel by Arab states, took over the hill and made it a kind of 'no man's land'. The Israelis tolerated this without ever accepting it. To this day, the task of UNTSO is to extend again and again the ceasefire agreements made after wars in the Middle East.

In Israel, vehement criticism is voiced about this seat of the United Nations organisation in Jerusalem, where approximately 400 civil and military staff from two dozen different countries work. There is, after all, no ceasefire to be monitored here, say the Israelis. Moreover, the rapidly expanding city urgently needs this site for new housing. Now the United Nations is accused of illegal construction. It is said that buildings have been erected and the historic 'governor's palace' has been renovated on this land, inaccessible to the public, without Israeli approval and without the issuance of any building permits. And yet, according to the entry in the land registry, this is Israeli state territory.

Address Al'ar Street, Talpiyot Mizrah, Jerusalem 9380261 | **Getting there** Bus 78, 203 or 204 to Armon ha-Natsiv UN Observers Headquarters / Daniel Yanovsky Street | **Hours** Closed to the public – accessible from the outside only | **Tip** Haoman 17 is Jerusalem's most famous nightclub. It is equipped with an excellent sound system for appearances by international DJs (open Thu & Fri nights, 17 Haoman Street, Talpiot, +972 2 6781658).

49 _ The Hinnom Valley

Nuns are the guardians of ancient tombs

This valley was often a place of fear. A gorge to the south of the Old City of Jerusalem, it was used in biblical times by the Canaanites to sacrifice children. The prophet Jeremiah condemned this cult in the Old Testament and prophesied that one day the valley would be called the 'Valley of Slaughter'.

Later, it was held to be the site where the Last Judgement would take place and the ungodly would be punished. According to this belief, the entrance to the underworld, to hell, is here. Jesus uttered warnings about this valley and, according to all four evangelists, spoke of Gehenna as the location of hell. Sinful people, the hypocritical Pharisees, would suffer punishments to body and soul here. Hinnom is 'the destiny of all those who are eternally damned; here will be assembled all whose mouths speak unseemly words and who make evil report of His magnificence. This will be the place of judgement', in the words of the scriptures of Enoch.

Today, this peaceful valley between the Temple Mount and the Mount of Olives, which merges into the Valley of Kidron, is a place of recreation with lawns and trees. Sometimes sheep graze on the meadows. There are, however, some definite signs of the dark legends associated with this valley.

On the rocky slopes to the south-west of Mount Zion are caves that were hacked out of the rock in the time after Christ as a place to bury the dead. The spot where the Greek Orthodox Monastery of St Onuphrius stands was, according to tradition, acquired for use as a cemetery for strangers with the 30 pieces of silver received by Judas Iscariot, the betrayer of Jesus. On this 'field of blood', as it was called, Judas is said to have been buried, having killed himself after his betrayal. In 1874, the monastery was built, partly integrating these tombs. Today, a small community of nuns take care of the graves.

Address Hinnoma Valley, Ge-Hinnom in Hebrew | Getting there Bus 1 or 83a to Khanyon Givati / Ma'ale HaShalom | Hours St Onuphrius Monastery, in summer Tue & Thu 9am–noon & 4–7pm, in winter 9am–noon & 3–5pm | Tip The biblical pool of Siloah was discovered by chance in 2004 during construction work. The pool, at which Jesus healed a blind man, was beneath the garden of the Greek Orthodox church, where the over 2,000-year-old steps to a water basin were found.

50__The History Cinema

A time machine to antiquity and back

For an exciting virtual trip through 3,000 years of the history of Jerusalem, take the 'Time Elevator' in the Mamilla shopping centre. The guide through this entertaining journey is the musical star Chaim Topol (the star of *Fiddler on the Roof*). Employing all kinds of optical and acoustic tricks and a mixture of theatre scenes, original films and images, the show brings to life the turbulent past of the city in just under 40 minutes.

The re-enacted key historical scenes from biblical times – with choruses by Verdi and the sounds of Mozart as a backdrop – are played by excellent Israeli and American actors. The commentary, at times humorous and even ironic, makes it easy to follow the frequently dramatic and warlike events depicted in this 'edutainment' programme. The audience facing the huge screen, wearing seatbelts, as their cinema seats move around and shake from time to time, and headsets (the soundtrack plays in various languages, including English), find themselves immersed in the eventful eras of the prophets, King David and King Solomon, in the periods when Solomon's Temple and the Second Temple were destroyed, in Roman times when Emperor Hadrian built the Aelia Capitolina on the ruins of Jerusalem, and in the age of the medieval crusades.

The multimedia tour of three millennia, which is not especially profound or critical, ends with authentic images showing the independence of modern Israel, the series of Arab-Israeli wars, and finally the reunification of Jerusalem following the Six-Day War. The show, which is absolutely suitable for children from the age of five, takes a respectful attitude towards all three monotheistic religions, and reflects the Israeli view of history. At irregular intervals, the Time Elevator screens other films using the same technology. Among these are a virtual journey into space and a description of our solar system.

Address 6 Yitshak Kariv Street, Jerusalem 9410606, +972 2 26248381, www.timeelevator.co.il |
Getting there Bus 13, 19, 104, 105, 108, 115, 284, 480 or 755 to Mamilla/Agron Street |
Hours Sun–Thu 10am–5.20pm, Fri 10am–2pm | Tip The Jaffa Gate leads from the New
City into the Christian Quarter. The way through the gate, built in 1538 by Suleiman I,
involves a 90-degree turn, a means of preventing sudden attacks. The square in front of the
gate, reached from the shopping centre, is popular with buskers and street artists.

51 The House of Issa 6

The Christian Arabs' basketball idol

'Issa is the name, basketball the game', says the writing on posters in the Christian Quarter near the Jaffa Gate. This is the neighbourhood in which a professional basketball player grew up who was successful in the leagues in Israel, Greece and the USA. He never became a big star, but at home he was an idol for some. The inscription on his parents' house is a reminder of the story of Issa Kassissieh, which also mirrors the modern fate of Christian Arabs in Jerusalem.

The son of a stonemason, Issa discovered his love of basketball at the age of nine. He used a car tyre that he suspended from the city wall as his basket. Sometimes he would entertain passers-by with his tricks and by juggling with balls. Issa trained hard, was talented and agile. As a young man, he soon became a member of the Palestinian national team. The Kassissiehs are a family with a long tradition – their name means 'relative of a priest' and are one of a declining number of Arab Christian families living in the Old City. They adored him, and posters bearing the words 'Issa 6' in front of the skyline of Jerusalem, showing the player balancing a basketball on his head, could be seen everywhere in the Christian Quarter in the late 1990s. His fans even scrawled 'We love you, Issa' on the walls of churches.

However, 'Issa 6' was never an idol for all Palestinians, although they are undoubtedly sports enthusiasts. Some people in Jerusalem believe this relates to his Christian background. In some places, slogans such as 'pray for the priests in Jerusalem' are on the house walls right next to messages of support for Issa 6. They draw attention to the growing problems that face the Christian minority.

Today, the man at the centre of this, who still neither drinks nor smokes, lives a fairly retired life in Jerusalem. He trains young basketball players, but the local club cannot pay him for this work.

Address 6 Greek Patriarchate Street, Jerusalem 97300 | Getting there Tram to City Hall,
enter through the Jaffa Gate – the second street on the left, seen from the gate | Tip The
Greek Orthodox Patriarchate Museum contains many holy relics, sarcophaguses, grave-
stones, lamps, relief sculptures, coins, icons, triptychs, chalices and priests' robes (Greek
Orthodox Patriarchate Road).

52___The Hungarian Shtetl

Living traditions in Beit Ungarin

At the heart of Mea Shearim is the quarter of Hungarian Jews. They played a considerable part in establishing Israel: the founder of Zionism, Theodor Herzl, was a Hungarian born in Budapest under the name Herzl Tivadar. Most of his Jewish compatriots were unenthusiastic about the idea of a Jewish state, but in the late 19th century many orthodox Jews from Hungary followed his call to the Promised Land.

Many of them found a new home in Mea Shearim. Until World War I, Beit Ungarin consisted of about 100 houses, a synagogue, a school and a bathhouse (mikvah). As the years passed, small workshops opened – carpenters, metalworkers or goldsmiths. Little has changed in the district since then, because Hungarian orthodox Jews believe that living a life pleasing to God involves, alongside obeying religious laws, trying to hold on to old traditions in everyday life, and above all keeping to strict rules for the Shabbat.

The weekly holy day is of outstanding importance for them. On Friday evening the Haredin, in their festive clothing of gold-coloured coats or striped kaftans, with broad fur caps or starched hats, pour into the synagogue singing and praying. They are accompanied by their wives in long, flowing dresses, wearing headscarves or wigs, and by their numerous offspring, also in their best clothes. And heaven help any ignorant person who drives a car through the quarter by mistake on the Shabbat. When this happens, Israeli soldiers often have to rescue cars that are surrounded by angrily shouting Haredin.

In Israel, the orthodox are not well-liked everywhere, if only because of their special privileges such as exemption from military service. In view of their high birth rate, Haredin will soon be the majority in Jerusalem. Especially as more than 1,000 young people leave Jerusalem every year in favour of pleasure-loving Tel Aviv.

Address In the middle of Mea Shearim, between Shivtei Israel Street, Shomrei Enumin Street and Mea Shearim Street, Jerusalem 9510552 | Getting there Tram to City Hall or Jaffa Center | Tip Two Hungarian restaurants, the last of their kind in Jerusalem, are close by: Sweet Moments Hungarian Glatt Kosher Dairy Food (Sun–Thu 10am–11pm, 19 Yo'el Moshe Salomon, +972 77 4002098) and Rega Matok (Sun–Thu 11am–9pm, 18 Yo'el Moshe Salomon).

53 The Immovable Ladder

For emergency supplies to the Holy Sepulchre

The wooden ladder above the entrance to the Church of the Holy Sepulchre is the most visible symbol of the bitter conflict among the Christian churches. The centuries-old disputes at the site of the crucifixion, entombment and resurrection of Christ have lost none of their acrimony to this day. For this reason, all parties comply with the *status quo*, which was last reviewed in 1853 under Ottoman rule. According to this, the Armenian Apostolic monastery has the right to the ladder that leads from an outer building to the right-hand double window above the entrance.

Why it is there, and how long it has been there, is a matter for debate. Drawings show that it was already in place in 1728. It was used by Armenian monks to supply themselves with food by raising a basket into the air whenever the Muslim rulers of the city, tired of the quarrelling among Christians, simply closed the church to all groups involved. The Armenians' right to the ladder means that it is simply replaced as soon as it has become rotten or damaged.

The conflict around the Church of the Holy Sepulchre, which was built in the 4th century and reconstructed following damage in the 11th century, is sparked mainly by the question of which Christian confession, out of the six represented there, may hold their services when and where. In 1757, the Turkish sultan in Istanbul, ruler of the Ottoman Empire, therefore issued a 'ferman' – a decree specifying responsibilities and rights in the church, with its many chapels, altars and shrines. This regulates, for example, the processions or the times of services. In the disagreements among the clergy, there have repeatedly been fights in which sometimes heavy candles or even crucifixes were employed as weapons.

The *status quo* may only be changed by the mutual consent of all. So the ladder will presumably stay where it is until the Day of Judgement.

Address Sukh el-Dabbagha, Jerusalem 9114002 | **Getting there** Tram to City Hall, then through the Jaffa Gate and via David Street and Christian Quarter Street to the Sukh el-Dabbagha | **Tip** The ceremonial opening and closing of the gate of the Church of the Holy Sepulchre is carried out at dawn and dusk by the Nusseibeh and Judeh families. As the Christians disagreed among themselves, Sultan Saladin gave these families the keys to the holy site more than 800 years ago.

54 Independence Park
Whitewater and beer festivals on disputed ground

Children in Jerusalem can play in many parks, on squares and in courtyards. But the facilities in Independence Park are much more attractive. Although signs prohibit bathing in the small pool of water with artificial springs and in the long artificial stream with its harmless rapids, on hot days crowds of boys and girls splash about here without their parents or anyone else trying to stop them. The second-biggest park in the city, centrally located right next to the Mamilla cemetery, is not only a favourite place for strolling, picnicking and snoozing, it is also used for big beer festivals, political demonstrations and cultural events.

For many years, nothing stood on this land, as until 1967 part of it was in the no man's land between the Israelis and the Jordanians, who controlled East Jerusalem. Even after the Six-Day War, when the Israelis were in command of the whole city, the city government hesitated for a long time to approve plans for the area. One reason for this was protests by Islamic authorities who were concerned about protecting Muslim graves. The site includes the 'Lion's Den', an important burial place associated with Jewish, Muslim and Christian legends.

After years of disputes and the preservation of a few Muslim graves, the park was finally finished in 1996. Since then it has been one of the most frequented green spaces in the city. Since 2005, one of the country's biggest beer festivals has taken place here over two days each summer. The Jerusalem Beer Festival, where 120 kinds of beer from local breweries and international brands are showcased, is usually attended by more than 15,000 people. After sunset, the park is livelier than most spots by the standards of the Holy City. There are live concerts on most evenings. The LBGT community and student theatre groups also use the park for their events and parties.

Address Agron Street, King George Street, Hillel Street and Menashe Ben Yisrael Street, Jerusalem 9426702 | Getting there Bus 13 or 19a to Tsarfat Square/Agron Street | Tip The imposing Great Synagogue holding 1,400 people was completed in 1982, based on the style of the ancient Jewish temple. In the lobby, a historical collection of mezuzahs, small capsules with biblical words for the door posts of Jewish houses, is displayed (56 King David Street, visiting times Sun–Thu 9am–1pm).

55 Ishtabach

Secret Kurdish recipes in the orthodox quarter

Oren Sasson-Levi's idea for making a living was to set up his own business using the favourite recipe of his grandmother, who came from Syrian Kurdistan. Today, Ishtabach, his eatery at the heart of the mainly orthodox quarter near the Mahane Yehuda Market, is a popular place to meet, especially for young people.

The house speciality is called 'siske'. This is a baked flatbread stuffed with spiced minced beef that has been braised for 15 hours, sweet potatoes, caramelised onions, sweet peppers and chimichurri. As well as various 'shamburaks', a kind of oriental empanada with a variety of hearty fillings, the dishes are served with garlic jam, house-brewed beer and Oren Sasson-Levi's home-distilled arak, which is extremely fruity. All of these things are kosher, of course. And there are also vegetarian versions on the menu.

The name of the restaurant means both 'praise the Lord' and 'a man who cooks'. Ishtabach, with its massive brick oven in the larger of the two rooms, is exactly the right place for night owls, as it does not usually close until the last guest has departed. Part of the philosophy of his restaurant for Oren Sasson-Levi is having a very friendly, warm-hearted atmosphere. He was born in Jerusalem and as a result of a lengthy, severe illness once spent two months in a coma. Now he wants to do more than feed people – he wants Ishtabach to be a joyful place where people quickly feel at ease and get to know one another.

Late in the evening, in this corner restaurant, which is a little hidden away in its neighbourhood, with its long tables and a few seats outside, people often sing. High-spirited and enthusiastic, the boss and the waiter or waitress then regularly belt out classic pop or rock songs with their customers – hits by the Bee Gees, Rolling Stones or Beatles. And when groups of young soldiers come, they sometimes sing patriotic songs.

Address 1 Hashikmah Street, Jerusalem 9432301, +972 2 6232997 | Getting there
Tram to Mahane Yehuda; bus 17, 18, 32, 66, 74, 78 or 202 to Mahane Yehuda/Agripas |
Hours Sun–Wed noon–1am, Thu noon–2am, Fri 11am–2pm, Sat 8pm–1am | Tip The
Tax Museum displays an unusual collection from the millennia-old history of taxation.
Visit by appointment only (42 Agripas Street, Jerusalem 9430125, +972 2 6257597).

56 Israel's Menorah

The symbol of the Jewish state facing the Knesset

On the broad square in front of the Israeli parliament stands the country's biggest menorah, the seven-armed candelabrum that features on the state coat of arms. The bronze sculpture facing the Knesset, 5 metres high and 4 metres wide, symbolically links the 4,000-year-old history of the Jews to their modern state. The menorah was a generous gesture by the United Kingdom to Israel in 1956. This 'gift from the oldest to the newest parliament' was funded by British parliamentarians, banks, companies and private donors.

It is the work of the British sculptor Benno Elkan. A Jewish artist from Dortmund in Germany, in 1935 he emigrated to London, as the Nazis had banned him from working. Originally Elkan wanted to place the menorah symbolically at the entrance to the harbour of Tel Aviv or Haifa, a reference to the Statue of Liberty in New York harbour. The British donors persuaded Elkan to adopt this new, equally important location.

On the branches of the menorah, 29 reliefs tell the history of the Jews – from the battle of David against Goliath and the exodus from Egypt to the revolt in the Warsaw ghetto and the foundation of the state of Israel. No symbol apart from the star of David is so closely connected with Jewish identity as the menorah. Its outstanding significance is made clear by the fact that, although all fires are forbidden on the Shabbat for strictly religious Jews, the rule does not apply to the oil lamps on the menorah. It represents the tree of life for Jews and stands for spiritual enlightenment, insight and the joy of life.

According to the Bible, God himself prescribed the seven-branched candelabrum for the Jews. As the Israelites travelled to the Promised Land, on Mount Sinai Moses received not only the Ten Commandments, but also instructions for holy ceremonies, of which the seven-branched, decorated candelabrum made from pure gold is part.

Address Kiryat Ben-Gurion, Jerusalem 91950, +972 2 6753337, www.knesset.gov.il |
Getting there Bus 7, 35 or 66 to Knesset | Tip The Knesset has impressive architecture and
many works of art in its corridors and rooms. In the largest room, next to the parliamentary
chamber, are 12 floor mosaics and 3 huge tapestries by the Franco-Russian artist Marc
Chagall showing motifs from the Old Testament and Jewish history.

57__The Jerusalem Model

Architectural art by Conrad Schick

In the ruins of Bethesda or David's City you can imagine what Jerusalem looked like in Solomon's times or under Roman rule – but only models of old Jerusalem reflect the former glory of the city, which has been destroyed many times. Among the finest models are those made by Conrad Schick (1822–1901). A German architect and archaeologist, he left various traces in Jerusalem: as an architect in the Mea Shearim and Rehovia districts, as well as in the German Colony. He is also regarded as one of the leading archaeologists of the 19th century in Jerusalem. As a maker of models of Jerusalem, Schick, who did an apprenticeship as a craftsman when he was young, had a worldwide reputation.

Major works by his hand are held at the Paulushaus in East Jerusalem, the historic pilgrims' hostel of the German Association of the Holy Land. It was used as an office building for a time in the period of British rule. In the small museum on the lower floor of this imposing building are models of the Temple Mount in different historical ages, both during antiquity and in the 19th century. The latter model of the Temple Mount and the Dome of the Rock was made by Schick as a commission from the Ottoman sultan. Schick's intricate work in wood attracted worldwide attention at exhibitions. The king of Württemberg bought a model of the Temple Mount and knighted Schick for his achievements. A viewing of these models is often included on the programme for official state visits to Jerusalem.

Schick, a pious Christian, loved Jerusalem. He came here as a missionary at the age of 24 and made a living by selling cuckoo clocks. His thirst for knowledge drove his self-taught studies of archaeology and architecture. He was involved in all important archaeological projects of his time, for example the discovery of the Siloam inscription in Hezekiah's Tunnel.

Address Paulushaus, 97 Nablus Road, Jerusalem 9119001, +972 2 6267800, www.heilig-land-reisen.de/paulushaus-haus | **Getting there** Tram to the Damascus Gate | **Hours** Mon–Sat 10am–5pm | **Tip** The daily market on Nablus Road is not as pretty as the Muslim shuk in the Old City, but the locals go there to buy fresh produce, spices, clothes, leather goods and household items, as well as plastic toy guns.

58 Kikar Hamusica

Free live concerts on the music square

Only a few years ago the Nahalat Shiva district in the city centre was unattractive and seemed somewhat neglected in places – until the French-Israeli businessman Laurent Levy bought up a large area, pulled down old buildings and with a considerable investment constructed a number of modern apartment blocks, the façades clad with lovely Jerusalem stone, as well as a lot of shops and the Museum of Jewish Music.

At the heart of this newly built complex Levy, a wealthy manufacturer of spectacles, built an architecturally fine square, called Kikar Hamusica, flanked by five restaurants and cafés and a stage with first-class equipment. This is now an important place for cultural encounters and a popular rendezvous for young people, where free concerts are given almost every day. These range from classical klezmer music, folk music and ballads to jazz, rock and classical music. Those who would like to enjoy the performances at the tables outside the elegant eateries on the square naturally have to order something.

In implementing his Kikar Hamusica project, the investor Laurent Levy had a vision for which he quickly gained supporters: in Jerusalem, where religions and cultures clash, he wanted to create a place for music, and thus for peace, that brings together people of different origins and faiths. Because there is nothing, he stressed, that makes connections between people better than music that moves the soul. For this reason, Levy also funded the Museum of Jewish Music at the rear of the square.

In the buildings around it are five places to eat, among them the celebrated gourmet restaurant Kinor Bakikar. There are plans to install a concert hall, a recording studio and schools for comedy, dance and music in the complex. The subject of music is also to be the dominant theme in the design of a hotel, planned for 2020. Levy's motto is 'Unite everyone with music!'

Address Beit David Street, Yoel Moshe Salomon Street and Maa'var Beit Haknesset, www.kikar-hamusica.com/en, Jerusalem 94633 | Getting there Tram to Zion Square, then walk to Yoel Moshe Salomon Street and take the second right into Beit David Street | Hours Concerts usually begin in the evening, at various times; the cafés have different opening times | Tip The Blue Hall Music is a basement bar in the complex at the corner of Salomon Street and Maa'var Beit Haknesset. It serves acclaimed food and has a long bar. On many evenings there is live music, especially reggae, funk, rock and hip-hop (12 Yoel Moshe Salomon Street, +972 2 6256488, Sun – Thu from 5pm, www.bluehallmusic.co.il).

59__ The Klezmer Cellar
Yiddish music and dancing at Bursteins

The clarinettist Avram Burstein has a mission. He devotes himself to the Yiddish tradition of classical klezmer music. Whereas many klezmer musicians experiment with elements of pop, reggae and jazz, or with modern instruments, the small, almost hidden-away cellar bar in the Romema district is the picturesque home of klezmer as it was played in the old Ashkenazy shtetls before the Holocaust. Theologically, the message of klezmer music, according to Burstein, stands for 'redemption'.

In the evening as Shabbat is drawing to a close, this grandson of a Polish immigrant celebrates the beginning of a new Jewish week with music, dance, traditional dishes such as chicken liver pâté and wine, and also with the words of the Torah. The composition of the musical ensemble often changes. Sometimes practitioners of klezmer arrive unexpectedly and make music together as in a jam session.

Burstein, a musician or even the cook dances with astonishing elegance, while balancing a glass or a bottle on his head, to the cheerful, infectious music. There is space for three dozen customers at the most in the cellar with its old-fashioned fittings, small stage, settees, chairs, armchairs and bookshelves full to bursting with Yiddish literature.

Guests are welcome, but should pay attention to the orthodox dress code. A small 'donation' of 25 shekels is requested for the performance, the Yiddish snacks and the drinks. There is no menu, and everything has an intimate atmosphere. Avram Burstein's cellar is his passion, rather than a business. Deeply religious, he supports his wife and five children mainly from the proceeds of tours of Europe and from performing at weddings and other festivities. Burstein's grandparents came to Israel from Poland in the 1930s. He proudly reports that the number of their children and their children's descendants now exceeds 1,000 persons.

Address 52 Yermiyahu Street, Jerusalem 9446733, +972 52 2879123 | **Getting there** Bus 55, 57, 64, 65 or 69 to Yirmiyahu / Elihav | **Hours** Winter, Sat from 9pm; summer, Sat from 10pm, or as announced | **Tip** On nearby Allenby Square is the British war memorial honouring Field Marshal Edmund Allenby, who conquered Jerusalem in 1917. The monument bears reliefs of medieval knights, thus linking his victory over the Turks to the Crusades.

60__The Lev Smadar Cinema
A bastion of secular citizens

Jerusalem's oldest cinema had to fight for survival at times. In 2017, this old-established picture palace, which puts on an ambitious programme of international films, usually in English or with English subtitles, was only saved when a citizens' initiative stepped in. The cinema was threatened with closure because its old building no longer complied with strict safety regulations. No money was available to renovate it. When this became known, an alliance of businesspeople, intellectuals and young people formed to campaign for the cinema and promoted season tickets. In the end, the operators of Lev Smadar, the owner of the building and the city authorities agreed on a compromise solution.

It belongs to the Lev chain of cinemas, which screen high-quality movies, often in combination with talks or panel discussions. The aim is to be a living example of cultural diversity, also showing Arab and Iranian films. In order to stay in business as an old-fashioned cinema, though with highly modern equipment, in the age of Netflix and YouTube, the operators have also invested in the restaurant and the bar in the spacious foyer.

The writer Gil Yaron described Lev Smadar as an 'atheists' temple of culture' and one of 'the last refuges of secular culture in the Holy City'. Here he was referring to the growing presence and influence of orthodox Jews.

The cinema was opened in 1928 under the name 'Orient' by a businessman from the German Templer community. After the Nazis seized power in Germany, the cinema was drawn into the vortex of political controversy in Jerusalem, and at the outbreak of war in 1939 the British authorities took over the building. Later, Israelis took control, and renamed it 'Smadar'. At first it was a movie house for cheap westerns and kitschy films. Its small auditorium, with seating for 200, was a popular spot for teenagers on their first dates.

Address 4 Lloyd George Street, Jerusalem 9311004, +972 2 5660954, www.lev.co.il/en |
Getting there Bus 18, 34, 77, 102, 103 or 108 to Emek Refaim Street / Lloyd George
Street | Hours Mon–Fri 3pm–midnight, Sat & Sun 10am–midnight | Tip Basher
Fromagerie in the German Colony stocks an enormous variety of cheeses, many of them
from France, Italy and other European countries. Tempting European wines and
imported delicacies are also sold here (52 Emek Refaim Street).

61 The Light Rail Train
A symbol of coexistence

Jerusalem has only one tram line, even though the city authorities have been planning new routes for a long time. But the L1 line is 14 kilometres long and connects Mount Herzl in the south-west with the district of Pisgat Ze'ev in the north-east of the city. For tourists who want to reach many parts of Jerusalem conveniently, the tram, which goes across the spectacular bridge designed by Calatrava, is a fantastic option. And the Light Rail Train is also the only place where all of the people of Jerusalem, regardless of their religion and origin, really meet regularly and often. The tram is seen as a symbol of coexistence.

More than 30,000 Arabs from the east of the city work in West Jerusalem and many of them use the tram. During the rush hour they crowd into the modern carriages, as do ultra-orthodox Jews in their black clothing, young female soldiers with their machine pistols strapped on, Muslim women wearing a headscarf or hijab, noisy teenagers with gaudy punk hair, Christian monks and nuns, and office workers in conservative suits. Every day the tram, which went into operation in 2011, peacefully unites Jerusalem's colourful, multicultural and divided society. Visitors are often surprised at the usually relaxed atmosphere in this city of conflict – something that is particularly noticeable in the trams. There was just one period when the trams and tram stops were targets for political vandalism. In the autumn of unrest in 2014, young Palestinians in the eastern part of the city threw stones at trams and damaged tram stops. An unusual feature of this transport system is the frequency of ticket checks. The reason is that only 23 vehicles operate in total. The inspectors are usually unbending, with tourists too. Tickets have to be bought from a machine before the journey. Those who do not stamp them in the carriage pay a hefty fine for fare-dodging.

Address Mount Herzl and Pisgat Ze'ev tram terminuses | **Getting there** Operating
Sun–Thu 5.30am–midnight, Fri 5.30am until one hour before start of Shabbat, Sat
30 minutes after sunset | **Tip** The Teddy Kollek Stadium holds 32,000 spectators, is
home to four football clubs, and is known as 'hell' (Gehinnom) because of the atmosphere
of the confined arena with roof. This atmosphere makes it worthwhile to attend a league
game (Malha district, David Ayalon Street, Jerusalem 96950).

62 __ The Lions Fountain

A gushing gift from Germany

Many different countries have donated buildings, monuments, parks or sculptures to the Holy City. The remarkable gift from the German government not only stands in a beautiful location in the Bloomfield Garden, but has also been visibly well received by the citizens of Jerusalem. In summer, families, lovers and strollers come to the Lions Fountain in the Bloomfield Garden. Children love to splash around in the fountain or climb on the bronze figures.

The work has now acquired a status as one of the landmarks of modern Jerusalem. In 1981, it was donated to the city, according to the official account at the suggestion of Helmut Kohl, chancellor of the Federal Republic of Germany. The large fountain near the King David Hotel, which has a radius of 10 metres, communicates a restrained message of peace that is only recognisable when you look more closely.

At the centre of the fountain stands a five-metre-tall 'Tree of Life', spurting jets of water, with three abstract, heavy, scrolled branches. As conceived by the artist Gernot Rumpf, from Rhineland Palatinate, they represent the three monotheistic religions, which live in peace together, surrounded by lions that spout water. The elegantly curved motif of the installation has in the meantime been used several times elsewhere by Rumpf, who made his reputation principally with works related to biblical themes, but all with a tongue-in-cheek sense of humour.

At the top of the multi-layered tree is a globe, on which there sits a dove with an olive branch in its beak. This is intended to represent the dove that Noah sent out after the Flood, which returned 300 days later bearing the branch, as a sign from God of reconciliation with humankind. On the broad surround of the fountain stand several bronze lions. At the feet of one of the big cats there is a small basin of water, from which bronze doves drink.

Address Bloomfield Garden, King David Street / Yemin Moshe Quarter, Jerusalem 94101 |
Getting there Bus 13, 18, 102, 105 or 108 to David HaMelekh / Mapu | **Tip** *Etzioni Flame*
is a metal sculpture in the Bloomfield Garden. This remarkably dynamic and lifelike
work by the Israeli sculptor Gidon Graetz commemorates the Etzion Brigade, which was
responsible for defending Jerusalem during the War of Independence.

63— The 'Little Western Wall'

A holy place in a narrow alley

Whereas prayers are offered day and night at the famous Western Wall, which is also a synagogue in part, the less well-known 'Little Western Wall' can often be found free of visitors – although according to Jewish beliefs it is equally one of the last remaining parts of the Jewish temple that was destroyed by the Romans in the year 70 CE. To this day, the remains of the western wall that protected the temple symbolise for Jews God's covenant with the people of Israel. In terms of its proximity – a point that is of decisive importance for some orthodox Jews – the Little Western Wall was even closer to the Holy of Holies in Herod's temple than the famous Western Wall, which is also known in English as the Wailing Wall.

The smaller wall, too, is regarded as a Jewish holy place, though it has only had this status for a century, and is now also a place of prayer. In contrast to the arrangements at the larger Western Wall, in front of the 2,000-year-old masonry in Bab al-Hadad Street, there is no separation of men and women. And here nobody pays attention to whether men wear a kippah or not.

In this narrow alley in the Muslim Old Town there are buildings from the Mamluk period (12th and 13th centuries). Its closeness to the Jewish holy site gives an impression of how things used to look near the Western Wall. After the Six-Day War in 1967, the square in front was greatly enlarged – and many houses belonging to Arabs near the Western Wall had to make way for this.

The orthodox Jewish organisation Ateret Cohanim has been campaigning for years for an improvement to the Little Western Wall, and wants it to be placed under the authority of the Israeli minister of religion. One reason for this may be that the wall, known to Muslims as the 'Kurdish hospice' (Ribat al-Kurd), has been subject to vandalism by young Palestinians.

Address At the end of Bab al-Hadad Street, next to the Iron Gate of the Temple Mount, Jerusalem 9114101 | **Getting there** Walk from the Damascus Gate along the Via Dolorosa into the Muslim quarter, in the direction of the Temple Mount | **Tip** The proper Western Wall (around the corner from the smaller one) is the most important Jewish holy place. In front of it are crowds of people who pray or place small slips of paper with their prayers and wishes into the joints of the wall. The dress code is strict: men and women must cover their heads.

64_ The Mamilla Passage

Masterpieces to decorate a luxury shopping mall

A remarkable art experiment outside the walls of museums and galleries, in the spirit of culture for everyday life as evoked by curators and culture managers, is taking place in the Mamilla shopping centre. On the 300-metre-long shopping street Alrov Mamilla Avenue, where the boutiques of major international brands, expensive jewellers, antique dealers and watch shops crowd together with galleries, cafés and restaurants, sculptors, most of them from Israel, present their works.

About 80 sculptures by 27 artists were assembled by the curator of this unusual exhibition, Tzipi Vital, for the summer season of 2018. The objects, made from various materials, both abstract and representational, examples of different styles of art, are for sale. Small signs refer to the gallery or artist. The exhibitions along the avenue of 140 shops, changing annually, match the unique complex that houses the shopping centre, luxury hotel and upmarket apartments.

Even construction work in Mamilla, once a poor district on the former ceasefire line between Israel and Jordan, was controversial, as it was necessary to resettle 700 families. To preserve the historic building fabric, before demolition of the dilapidated old houses, all the stones of the façades were numbered, then reused when the modern complex was built of pale Jerusalem stone at the beginning of this century. Several buildings were even completely integrated. One of them is the Stern Building, in which the Zionist Theodor Herzl resided in 1898 when he visited Jerusalem. Today, it is occupied by a bookshop and a high-class restaurant. Then there is the impressive monastery of St Vincent de Paul, built in the late 19th century. The oldest structure on the Mamilla site, it consists of a church, the main building with the convent and facilities for people with handicaps, and 16 shops on the pedestrian zone.

Address Mamilla Mall, Shlomo HaMelech Street / Itzchak Kariv Street, Jerusalem 94182, www.alrovmamilla.com | Getting there Tram to City Hall; bus 13, 104, 108 or 115 to Mamilla Mall | Hours Sun–Thu 10am–11pm, Fri 9.30am–3pm, Sat after end of Shabbat until 11pm | Tip In the Citadel of David behind the Jaffa Gate lies an archaeological park where in the evenings a three-dimensional light show about the history of Jerusalem is displayed with exciting colour and light effects. Images, collages and film scenes with a backdrop of heroic music are projected onto the walls, ruins and buildings (+972 2 6265333; Mon & Wed 8.30pm, Thu 9.30pm, Sat 9pm but subject to change).

65__ The Montefiore Windmill

A symbol of early Zionism that almost never turned

Legends surround this 19th-century structure. Arab building workers are said to have tried to sabotage the project and to have put a curse on it. It was long believed that the mill never went into operation, but now it is known that it carried out its task for a few years at least. This is no longer the case, as the mill, built in 1857 and based on British models, does not get enough wind in its valley. Moreover, the grain that was harvested here was harder than grain grown in England, so the machinery was unsuitable.

The banker, businessman and philanthropist Sir Moses Montefiore ordered its construction. Although it had little economic success, it became a striking symbol of Zionism. Montefiore made a large fortune and attained considerable renown as a young man in London thanks to his success in business. He was the first British Jew to be ennobled as a baronet. In 1827, at the age of 40, he travelled to Palestine. After that journey, he became strictly observant in his faith and an ardent Zionist.

Montefiori, who was over six feet tall and lived to the age of 99, later withdrew from his business activities in London and began to promote the project of a Jewish state by building printworks, factories, schools and hospitals in Palestine. He founded the first Jewish settlement, Mishkenot Shaananim, outside the Old City. The 18-metre-high windmill, built to provide work and ensure the supply of bread for a few brave settlers outside the city walls, became its conspicuous landmark.

During the War of Independence, the windmill gained a certain significance, when it was used by Jewish snipers. This caused the British army to attack the mill, a measure that they fittingly named 'Operation Don Quixote'. Since 2012, the windmill has been functional again following restoration. Now it demonstrates the traditional milling of grain to school pupils and tourists.

Address Sderot Blumfield, Yemen Moshe Quarter, Jerusalem 9108102, +972 2 6292220 |
Getting there Bus 13, 105 or 108 to David HaMelekh / Mapu | Hours Museum Sun – Thu
9am – 4pm, Fri 9am – 1pm | Tip The Sultan's Pool is an ancient water reservoir, now used
as an amphitheatre with 10,000 seats. The reservoirs, 12 metres deep and covering an area
as large as two football pitches, were part of the water supply to Jerusalem from antiquity
until the 20th century. Concerts and performances now take place here.

66 The Museum on the Seam

A cultural project for Israelis and Arabs

The aim of this unique museum is to serve peace, reconciliation and dialogue, using contemporary art as a medium to explain and overcome boundaries and conflicts, to respect and accept our fellow human beings. Symbolically it is housed in a building that was once an Israeli military post; a large number of bullet holes on the façade of this Arab villa, built in 1932, testify to the battles of the Six-Day War. Until 1967 this was also the site of the Mandelbaum Gate, then the only crossing point between Jewish West Jerusalem and Arab East Jerusalem.

Political, religious, economic and ethnic diversity and divisions, not only in this region but also globally, are the background to the changing exhibitions. Images, montages, sculptures, art installations and multimedia presentations are devoted to such topics as migration, prejudice, violence and slavery. Works by artists from the Arab world and Iran are also shown. Raphie Etgar, head of the museum since it opened in 1999, knows that the art exhibited here is often neither easy to look at nor aesthetically pleasing, but is at times upsetting and disturbing.

The independent museum, which is not funded by the state, has an attractive roof-top café, and is visited by both orthodox Jews and Palestinians. The project began on the initiative of the former mayor of Jerusalem, Teddy Kollek, and the German publisher Georg von Holtzbrinck, whose family ensured the financing until recently – the income earned from some 15,000 visitors per year is not enough to cover the costs.

Although *The New York Times* has named the museum one of the '29 leading places of art in the world', and many teachers in the city arrange visits with their classes as part of their standard programme, the institution, which has often been praised by politicians, for example by the president of Israel, is now fighting for survival due to lack of money.

Address 4 Chel Handasa Street, Jerusalem 910160, +972 2 6281278, www.mots.org.il |
Getting there Tram, bus 3, 17, 19 or 66 to Shivtel Yisrael | Hours Mon, Wed, Thu
10am – 5pm, Tue 2 – 8pm, Fri 10am – 2pm | Tip Some Anglican and free-church
Christians believe that the ancient burial site known as the Garden Tomb is the grave
of Jesus. This burial chamber from the Roman period was cut from a rock wall several
metres high, and is surrounded by a well-tended, pretty garden (Conrad Schick Street,
Mon – Sat 8am – 6pm).

67__The Music Museum

Oriental splendour and a virtual journey

The most exciting surprise in this interactive music museum is only marginally related to the subject of its wonderful multimedia display of historic instruments. After visitors have passed through seven rooms, each of them entirely different in its decoration and fittings, and each reflecting a period of cultural history, there awaits a plain-looking room with headsets.

With these you can immerse yourself with unbelievable intensity in the world of King Solomon, exploring the first holy temple of the Jews with its Torah ark and the Ark of the Covenant. This virtual journey back to ancient times enables you to swivel the view of the palace by 360 degrees and pay attention to the details that are of particular interest. A small orchestra accompanies this virtual trip into the Jewish past with the sounds of historic instruments.

A fascinating aspect of the Hebrew Music Museum is its successful recreation of the atmosphere of different periods of history using furnishings, colours and shapes. In addition to the impressive collection of almost 300 musical instruments, there are also many interactive exhibits that enable visitors to soak up more intensely a musical history going back 2,500 years and traditions since the days of Babylonian exile. In 2016, a private investor spent more than €10 million on the museum, which was built without assistance from the state.

On entering the museum, visitors are given a choice of a guided tour or can take a tablet computer and a headset that takes them through the exhibition, with a choice of various languages. And the expensively fitted museum shop is astonishing for its huge stock of figures, objects, replicas, photos and historic recordings ranging across the history of music – not only Jewish music. This shop is a treasure trove for gifts and souvenirs – some of them not cheap – with connections to music.

Address 12 Yo'el Moshe Salomon Street, Jerusalem 9463312, +972 72 3281976, www.facebook.com/musicmuseumjerusalem | Getting there Tram to Zion Square, then turn into Yo'el Moshe Salomon Street (pedestrian zone) | Hours Sun–Thu 9.30am–8pm, Fri 9.30am–1.30pm | Tip Yo'el Moshe Salomon Street in front of the museum is an attractive alley, above which hundreds of colourful opened umbrellas are hung in summer. A pedestrian street, it is full of shops selling art, souvenirs and knick-knacks, jewellers, galleries, small cafés and restaurants.

68 The National Concert Hall
A temple for the art of music

The place in Jerusalem where stars and legends of music, ballet and dance take the stage is the Henry Crown Hall. It is the second-largest of six auditoria in the Jerusalem Centre for the Performing Arts, Israel's leading arts centre, whose architecture resembles a hostile fortress of pale Jerusalem stone. The largest space in this bulky building in the Talbieh district is reserved for theatre performances, usually in Hebrew. But the 760-seater concert hall is used to present the high art of music, from classical to jazz and folk. This hall is also the home of the renowned Jerusalem Symphony Orchestra.

The wide-ranging programme often concentrates on contemporary music, especially music from Israel, in addition to classical works by Mozart, Beethoven or Tchaikovsky. The relatively small symphony orchestra, an ensemble of about 80 musicians, has held world premières here of works by such composers as Sofia Gubaidulina, Henri Dutilleux and Alfred Schnittke.

The concert hall is named after a man who was more interested in football and sports than music. In the 1960s, the millionaire Lester Crown from Chicago donated nine million dollars for a new sports stadium in Jerusalem that was never built. Jerusalem's mayor at that time, Teddy Kollek, persuaded Crown to give all of the money to a cultural project instead. The arts centre was opened in 1971, and its large concert hall was named after the patron Crown, the third-largest auditorium after his wife Rebecca, and a wing of the building after his parents. The large theatre, however, was given the name of another donor, the industrialist Miles Sherover.

Thanks to multiple auditoria with performances taking place simultaneously, in the evenings the arts centre is also a lively place where people of different generations and widely divergent interests come together.

Address 20 Marcus Street, Jerusalem 91040, +972 2 5605755, www.jerusalem-theatre.co.il | Getting there Bus 13 to BeitHaNasi/Islam Museum | Tip The L.A. Mayer Museum for Islamic Art holds a highly unusual collection of clocks. Alongside art, jewellery, weapons and musical instruments from various eras of Islamic art, there are also performances of theatre and music, as well as workshops for adults and children (2 Hapalmach Street, +972 2 5661291, Mon – Wed 10am – 3pm, Thu 10am – 7pm, Fri & Sat 10am – 2pm).

69 The Neo-Kabbalist

Secret messages from the Torah in an orthodox home

If you would like to learn the secrets of the Bible, you have to climb 44 steps to the apartment of Avraham Levitt. A scholar and formerly an IT specialist in the USA, since 1997 he has lived with his large family in a modern house in the Jewish Quarter. His study on the upper floor is crammed with books, piles of papers and drawings. When he gives his talks in English, sometimes on the terrace with a view of the Western Wall, it is not unusual for small children to come crawling in, just as the bustling activity of modestly clad women in the kitchen is a normal state of affairs in this hospitable orthodox home.

What is at stake here is a bold school of thought. Levitt is a proponent of the New Kabbalah, a movement that aims to combine traditional Jewish mysticism with modern rational thinking. Its scholars believe that in this way they can find messages in the Torah that have previously been unknown. With the help of digital technology and by dispensing with the traditional way of reading – in Hebrew from right to left – they wish to discover new meaning. Some texts are also read from top to bottom and analysed.

Indeed, unbelievable revelations do emerge. As an example, Levitt cites the story of creation. The first book of Moses states that 'God said, let there be light, and there was light'. When he examines the text vertically, Levitt discerns strictly geometrical figures whose letters produce the words Bin Laden, attack, twin towers, murderers and thousands. He believes that this is a biblical reference to the terrorist attack on 11 September, 2001.

He and his teacher, the respected professor of mathematics Eliyahu Rips, see themselves as pioneers of a new kind of Torah research. Rips believes that he and the scientist Doron Witztum have discovered a 'Bible code'. However, at present, they say they are only at the beginning of this research.

Address 30 Misgav Ladach Street, Jerusalem 9751548, +972 58 6403066, www.whycodes.com |
Getting there Access to the Jewish quarter via the Jaffa Gate or Damascus Gate | Hours
By arrangement, talks for groups Sun–Thu 2pm | Tip The five villas from the period of the
Second Temple, today an archaeological museum with ritual baths and bathhouses decorated
with mosaics, are nearby in Hakara'im Street. The houses were destroyed during the Jewish
rebellion against the Romans in 70 CE (1 Hakara'im Street).

70__Nocturno

Nightlife with live music, poetry slam and art

Nocturno is a hotspot for young people in Jerusalem. During the day this lovingly furnished, cosy café-restaurant attracts customers with its stylish basket chairs and tables out in front on the broad pavement, which is partly covered. Guests who want peace and quiet while they drink coffee or eat lunch retire to the large room with a long bar on the lower floor, where a smoker's compartment is separated by glass partitions.

On the first floor at Nocturno there are exhibitions of art that change monthly, a spacious shop with creative products from Israeli studios, and exhibitions by young designers and craft workers. Some of them, including a goldsmith and a leather designer, have their studios in Nocturno. In corners stand settees and armchairs, or small conference tables for meetings, workshops and all kinds of talks. Many of the regulars and other guests are active in local politics.

In the evenings, Nocturno turns into a vibrant club with live music, performances or perhaps a poetry slam. There is something on the programme almost every evening. Amit Magal-Shlechter, the owner of Nocturno, who studied psychology and music theory, regards himself as a champion of the local scene and an arts manager, aiming not only to promote young musicians and artists but also to strengthen the 'liberal and pluralistic' side of Jerusalem. That is why his café also opens on the Shabbat – as late as 4am. For some regulars it has become a home from home where they often spend the entire day at their laptops. Nocturno wants to be 'funky and cosy at the same time', says Magal-Shlechter.

At the bars on the ground floor and in the cellar, several kinds of draught beer and a large selection of spirits are available. The menu is ambitious: it includes Israeli and Middle Eastern classics and newer creations as well as a wide range of vegetarian and vegan dishes.

Address 7 Bezalel Street, Jerusalem 9459107, +972 77 7008510, www.facebook.com/pg/Nocturnojerusalem | Getting there Bus 7, 18, 75 or 78 to Bezalel/Trumpeldor | Hours Sun–Thu 7am–midnight, Fri 7–4am, Sat 7.30am–midnight | Tip Less than 100 metres further on is the mural *Around the World in 92 Days* by the naïve artist Gabriel Cohen. This triptych on the façade of the Gerard Behar Center (scene of the trial of Eichmann in 1961) is a lively world scene depicting landmarks such as the Dome of the Rock, the Eiffel Tower, the Taj Mahal and the Pyramids of Giza (11 Bezalel Street).

71 Notre Dame

A Vatican base with a famous church

The massive building with a large statue of the Virgin Mary above the main façade almost looks like a castle dominating the Old City. In fact, the Notre Dame of Jerusalem Center was for many years the unofficial representation of the Vatican in the Holy Land. Before Israel and the Holy See established diplomatic relations in 1994, the head of this luxurious hostel was considered a kind of ambassador of the Vatican in Jerusalem. For almost 20 years this was the legendary Monsignor Richard Mathes, a German Catholic priest from the Ruhr area, a highly educated and polyglot man who enjoyed great respect internationally for his impartiality.

For more than 100 years, Notre Dame, which was previously owned by a male religious order, the Assumptionists, has been used as a hostel for pilgrims. It suffered severe damage in the Arab-Israeli fighting, and only flourished again after the Israeli occupation of East Jerusalem in 1967 and the acquisition of the building by the Vatican in 1972. Visitors feel as if they have entered a five-star hotel, not only because of the large lobby with fine furnishings and works of art, or the gourmet restaurant.

For church dignitaries and well-heeled pilgrims, Notre Dame is the address of choice in Jerusalem. In its comfortable rooms, they have WiFi but no television. Priests are available round the clock for a talk or for confession. Special attractions are the shroud exhibition, the chapel designed in bright colours by the French artist Jean Cocteau, and the highly acclaimed cuisine. The rooftop restaurant, which specialises in cheese and wine, commands a superb view of the Old City. The modern 500-seater auditorium was inaugurated by Pope John Paul II in the year 2000. Notre Dame is run by a Mexican religious order, the Legionaries of Christ. The hotel school plays an important role in the training of young Palestinians.

Address 3 HaTsanhanim, Jerusalem 9120402, +972 2 6279111, www.notredamecenter.org |
Getting there Tram to City Hall; bus 17, 19a, 30, 49 or 66 to Min'heret Tzahal /
HaTzankhanim | Tip The richly decorated Church of the Saviour with its beautiful organ
and the Franciscan Saviour Monastery stand opposite Notre Dame in the Christian Quarter
of the Old City. The monastery was founded in 1551, the church in 1885 with the help of
Emperor Franz Joseph of Austria (1 St Francis).

72 — Palazzo Vecchio
A ministry in an Italian Renaissance building

The architecture of this magnificent building carried a political message. Constructed between 1911 and 1917, the Italian Hospital in the style of the Florentine Renaissance was intended to underline Italy's presence in the Holy Land – and other countries made demonstrations of their importance at that time by means of their domestic architecture.

The main building of the former hospital and the slender, 26-metre-high bell tower are clear references to the city hall of Florence, the majestic Palazzo Vecchio. The style of the chapel is more Gothic, with elements reminiscent of those present in Venetian architecture. The façades are adorned with motifs and emblems of Italian regions and cities such as Saint George slaying a dragon and the Roman she-wolf with Romulus and Remus.

The eminent Roman architect Antonio Barluzzi and his brother Giulio impressively succeeded in transplanting a piece of Italy into the urban scene of Jerusalem on the historic Street of the Prophets with a building that remains to this day one of the most beautiful in the city. Antonio Barluzzi (1884–1960) gained a reputation as the 'architect of the Holy Land', as he designed several chapels and churches, for example the pilgrimage church in the Garden of Gethsemane and the Calvary Chapel in the Church of the Holy Sepulchre.

The 100-bed Italian Hospital was originally run by nuns, and quickly earned great respect. However, the influence of Italy in the Holy Land did not noticeably increase. In World War I the Ottoman authorities occupied the clinic and in World War II it was requisitioned by the British air force. During the War of Independence, Zionist underground fighters used the building as an advance stronghold in battling the Jordanian army. In 1963, the state of Israeli bought the hospital and converted it into the Ministry of Education and Culture.

Address 29 Shivtei Israel Street, Jerusalem 9510552 | **Getting there** Tram, bus 17, 19 or 66 to Shivtel Yisrael | **Tip** The historic Tabor House with its tower, small church and pretty courtyard was built in 1882 by the archaeologist, missionary and architect Conrad Schick. It combines various architectural styles, and is now the seat of the Swedish Theological Institute.

73 _ Perfuniq
A workshop for personalised perfumes

This shop is more than a perfumery. It is also an open workshop where customers are playfully involved in creating a special scent that is guaranteed to be unique. A 'perfume for your personality', as the proprietor of Perfuniq, Shahar Schwartz promises.

Sitting on a bar stool, surrounded by hundreds of test tubes, phials and bottles containing aromatic oils, essences and other ingredients, customers begin by answering a few discreet questions put by the staff or the owner. Often, they are men who want to take an original gift home for their wife or girlfriend, and therefore have to start by describing her: what season of the year, what colour does she prefer, what does she like to eat? Does she have allergies? Does she like spicy food? Schwartz and his employees want to get a general impression first, in order to then compose a perfume directly tailored to the recipient, in cooperation with the customer.

On the basis of the interview, a selection of a considerable number of substances in dark glass vessels is made. Then the purchaser sniffs at dozens of sample scents on slender strips of paper, interrupting the process now and again by drinking a glass of water or eating a coffee bean, which neutralise and refresh the sense of smell. The question put to customers for each essence is simply how much they like it. When after half an hour or so the number of glasses and bottles has been reduced, about a dozen different ingredients remain, from which the perfumer finally makes the individual perfume.

A large number of perfume bottles with various designs are available for holding the newly created product. The customer also decides on a name and the type of lettering, as well as the packaging of the gift. Schwartz assures his clients that his shops in Jerusalem and New York are the only ones in the world that offer a perfume service of this kind.

Address 24 Ben Sira Street, Jerusalem 9418118, +972 52 4443900, www.perfuniq.com |
Getting there Bus 13, 19 or 387 to Mamilla/Agron Street | Hours Sun–Thu
11am–11pm, Fri 11am–3pm | Tip The Mamilla Cemetery is a historic Muslim burial
ground in which companions of the prophet Mohammed are said to have been laid to
rest in the 7th century. Only parts of the old cemetery remain, including the tomb of
Emir Aidughi Kubaki and several sufi shrines (Gershon-Agron Street).

74__The Puzzle Shop
Israeli brain-teasers

The small basement store with its building-block kits, wooden figures and board games might easily be mistaken for a nice-looking toy shop. But the customers here are not usually children. The business model at Gaya is founded on their interest in 'the art of thinking'. Its products are also aimed at children, but teenagers and young people seem to be the main groups who want to tackle its challenges.

More than 1,000 puzzles, board games and other thought games, all devised in Israel and made by hand from wood or other materials, are sold by Gaya. A specialist for mental exercise, the company now has seven branches across the country. In an age of computer games and virtual worlds, the Israeli market, as the owners of Gaya expected, has proved to be the ideal field for traditional board games and also for complex brain-teasers and games that test dexterity.

No country in the world has won more Nobel Prizes than Israel in relation to the size of its population. More than a fifth of all holders of a Nobel Prize in history are Jews – yet their proportion of the world population is only 0.2 per cent. The Jews regard themselves as the people of the book – meaning primarily the Torah, the word of God. The exceptional contribution made by Jews to the arts and sciences is undisputed.

Since 1997 Gaya has based its success on Israeli inquisitiveness. This small company promises its customers that they will have fun but also and above all intellectual stimulation, exercise for a healthy brain and 'a magic feeling of winning and satisfaction' on solving a difficult puzzle or mental task. Gaya stresses that all products comply with the highest American and European environmental standards. The company also holds workshops for creativity training and games of intelligence at different levels of ability, as well as play circles for two- and three-dimensional puzzles.

Address 7 Yo'el Moshe Salomon Street, Jerusalem 9463307, +972 2 6251515,
www.gaya-game.com, www.facebook.com/pages/gaya-the-art-of-thinking | Getting
there Tram to Zion Square, then turn into Yo'el Moshe Salomon Street (pedestrian
zone) | Hours Sun–Thu 10am–10pm | Tip Piccolino, an Italian-Israeli restaurant, puts
its faith in natural ingredients and its own recipes. The owners, the Dahan family, are
patriotic, and serve Israeli soldiers without a family free of charge every Friday (12 Yo'el
Moshe Salomon Street, +972 2 3281965, Sun–Thu 10am–11pm, Fri 10am–2pm).

75__ The Pyramid
Great architecture, suspected of Freemasonry

The Supreme Court is seen as an architectural masterpiece. *The New York Times* described this post-modern building with elements of Byzantine and Islamic style as Israel's most beautiful public building. The court is held in high regard, partly because it does not hesitate to curb the power of the government and army. It stopped the expulsion of African refugees and controversial tactics used by the army against terrorists. But the court is also the subject of conspiracy theories that are founded even in the acclaimed architecture of its building.

A gift to Israel by Dorothy de Rothschild, the court building is pervaded by magic symbols of the Freemasons and the Illuminati, according to these theories. Diabolical lines of force are said to link it to the Knesset, the central bank and the Rockefeller Museum. Above all, it is claimed, the pyramid on the roof, with round windows and the eye of God like the symbol that appears on American dollar bills, proves that the Illuminati are at work here.

When it opened in 1992, architecture critics praised the complex design of the well-lit building, a work by the architect Ram Karmi, an exponent of Brutalism (i.e. using bold swathes of exposed concrete), and his sister Ada Karmi-Melamede from Tel Aviv. They were trying to create connections to the Bible. At the entrance, a fine mosaic from an ancient synagogue was installed. The three-storey library is also fascinating. But for adherents of conspiracy theories, the contrasts used inside the building – of old and new, light and shade, wide and narrow – are merely more 'occult symbols' of the Antichrist.

The Supreme Court is situated between the prime minister's residence and the Knesset, which are directly connected to it through a walkway. This is intended to symbolise the link between the judiciary, the legislature and the executive in a democracy.

Address Kiryat Ben-Gurion, 1 Shaare Mishpat Street, Jerusalem 9195001, +972 77 2703333, www.elyon1.court.gov.il | **Getting there** Bus 7, 7a, 14 or 66 to Knesset | **Hours** Mon, Tue & Thu 8am–4pm, Wed & Sun 8am–6pm, Fri 8am–noon, guided tours in English Sun–Thu at noon | **Tip** The small museum in the Supreme Court has many documents and items from the periods of Ottoman rule and the British Mandate, as well as from the recent past.

76__The Qubbat al-Arwah
Mosque of ghosts for the Last Judgement

The small, octagonal domed building supported by eight slender columns has multiple significance in the Muslim world. According to an Islamic tradition, the souls of pious Muslims assemble here at night to pray, and Mohammed is said to have spoken to the biblical prophets of the Old and New Covenant here. Finally, it is said, the souls of believers will gather here on the day of the Last Judgement. Jews believe that the Qubbat al-Arwah, which is also known as the Dome of the Spirits and the Dome of the Winds, stands on the exact site of the Second Temple. At certain, specified times, Jews are allowed to visit this Islamic place of prayer.

The Dome of the Spirits, built above the oldest surviving mihrab (a prayer niche indicating the direction of Mecca) is at the northwestern end of the huge terrace on which the Dome of the Rock and the Al Aqsa Mosque stand. A detached structure with a heavy, semispherical dome, its base is a monolithic white slab of stone.

Nothing is known for certain about the history of the Qubbat al-Arwah: it is not clear who built it or why. There is speculation that a wealthy Islamic donor caused its construction and wished to remain anonymous. The first written mention of the building, which probably dates from the early 15th century, derives from Muhammad Agha, the administrator of the Holy Sites of the sultanate in the 17th century. His notes refer to the oil lamp in the mihrab and its maintenance.

For non-Muslim visitors, strict rules apply for visits to the Holy Sites of Islam in Jerusalem. In 2017 and 2018, access to the Dome of the Rock and the Al Aqsa Mosque was largely prohibited for non-Muslims. The Dome of the Spirits and the large square on which more than one million Muslims sometimes assemble for prayers on Fridays are freely accessible at certain times and through specified entrances.

Address Temple Mount, Muslim quarter, Jerusalem 9114101 | Getting there Tram
to the Damascus Gate, beyond the gate turn into El Wad Street | Hours Winter,
12.30am−10.30am & 12.30am−1.30pm; summer, 8.30−11.30am & 1.30−2.30pm |
Tip The Dome of the Rock and the Al Aqsa Mosque are magnificent buildings. The
Dome of the Rock, constructed in the 7th century and one of the most important
buildings of the Islamic world, is thought by Jews to be the site of the stone on which
the world was founded and Abraham wanted to sacrifice his son.

77__Rachel's Tomb

A Jewish holy place like a high-security prison

There are few other places where the bitter conflict between Israelis and Palestinians is as tangible as at this synagogue, the site of Rachel's tomb. At the edge of Bethlehem, it is heavily guarded by Israeli soldiers between concrete walls 10 metres high, and surrounded by barbed-wire fences. According to written evidence from the first centuries after Christ, this is the site of the tomb of the favourite wife of the Jewish patriarch Jacob, the mother of 2 of his 12 sons.

Jews traditionally pray at Rachel's tomb for their wishes to be fulfilled and ask for help with special needs. Rachel's tears are said to work miracles, so the faithful ask her to cry and thus intercede with God on their behalf. Women pray here for fertility. The small domed building with an old olive tree in front of it has been a symbol of Jewish identity for at least 1,700 years.

In 2010, the United Nations cultural organisation UNESCO approved an application by Islamic countries to describe the tomb on the list of World Heritage sites as a mosque with a double name in Arabic and Hebrew: 'Bilal Bin Rabah Mosque / Tomb of Rachel' is the name of the third-holiest site of Judaism according to this ruling. The Israeli government reacted with outrage, and in 2017 carried out its threat of withdrawing from UNESCO, as the USA had already done, accusing the organisation of blatant bias and hostility to Israel.

The mausoleum that can be seen today has been rebuilt a number of times. It derives from the Ottoman period and was erected on the ground of a Christian and Muslim cemetery. When the Zionist pioneer Moses Montefiore acquired the right to hold the keys in 1841 for the Jewish community, he had an Islamic prayer niche added to allay the fears of Muslims that the Jews might appropriate the tomb entirely – because it is regarded as a holy place by Muslims, as it is also by Christians.

Address Hebron Road, Bethlehem | Getting there Bus 163 and special buses by travel companies leaving from various places, usually hotels | Hours Sun–Wed 12.30am–10.30pm, Thu open 24 hours, Fri three hours before the Shabbat, Sat one hour after the end of the Shabbat | Tip The Palestine Museum of Natural History, 300 metres away, presents regional fauna and flora, and modern ecological projects. It is part of the Palestine Institute for Sustainability and Biodiversity at the University of Bethlehem (+972 2 2773553, daily 8am–8pm).

78__The Railway Bridge
Cattle trucks in Yad Vashem recall the horror

The Reichsbahn rail truck stands on a bridge that leads into the void. At the end of the track there is only an abyss. This is an extremely disturbing memorial to the inhuman mass deportations to Nazi concentration camps. The cattle truck at the Yad Vashem Holocaust Remembrance Center is a reminder that, of the six million Jews who were murdered, about one and a half million died during transportation. The sick, the old and the children were the ones who could not stand the strains of the journey in trucks that were crammed to the sliding doors and had no windows. Many of the humiliated, tormented deportees were even forced to pay for a 'ticket' to the death camps in Auschwitz and Treblinka.

Yad Vashem, Israel's central remembrance centre for the Holocaust, recalls the horror of the Shoa in various ways. The place to which all official visitors are taken is the Hall of Remembrance, where an eternal flame burns in the form of a broken bronze cup to commemorate the victims of the Holocaust. Beneath the stone slab are the ashes of the murdered, taken from German concentration camps. The names of the 22 largest camps are engraved in the floor.

Among the sculptures, monuments and other places of commemoration, the Memorial to the Deportees stands out with its raw, banal directness. It is a piece of everyday reality of the Holocaust, almost tangible, and upsetting. On the adjoining wall of the memorial is an inscription in both Hebrew and English recalling the testimony of a survivor of the Holocaust, Avraham Krzepicki.

The 12 years of Nazi rule in Germany not only brought about the most horrific break with civilisation of modern times, but also contaminated for ever many German objects, places and words in a disturbing way. To this day, at the sight of German cattle trucks, memories of this murderous period obtrude into the thoughts, not only of Jews.

Address Yad va-Shem Street, Jerusalem 9103401, +972 2 6443400, www.yadvashem.org |
Getting there Tram, bus 10, 16, 20, 23, 24, 26, 26a, 27, 27a, 28, 28a, 29, 33, 25, 39 or 150
to Mount Herzl, free shuttle bus to the memorial | **Hours** Mon–Wed 8.30am–6pm, Thu
8.30am–8pm, Fri 8.30am–2pm | **Tip** The summit of nearby Mount Herzl (834 metres)
is a park and a site for state commemorations. The national cemetery here is the burial site
of Theodor Herzl, founder of modern Zionism, and the prime ministers Shimon Peres,
Yitzhak Rabin and Golda Meir. At the entrance is a Theodor Herzl Museum.

79_Razzouk Ink

Tattoos for pilgrims for 700 years

As long ago as the 14th century, the ancestors of Wazzim Razzouk marked the skin of pilgrims in Jerusalem with symbols of their faith. Whereas tattoos are taboo for religious Jews and Muslims, some early Christians used this method of bearing witness to their new faith. During the Crusades, knights from the West had themselves tattooed so that if they died fighting, they could be identified on the battlefield and given a Christian burial. Since the time of the Crusaders, for many Christians a religious tattoo has been one of the duties of a pilgrimage to the Holy Land.

At Razzouk Ink, not far from the Jaffa Gate, this tradition has lived on for more than 700 years thanks to the Coptic Christian Razzouk family, who once immigrated from Egypt. In their small, technically modern tattoo salon, decorated with historic photographs and newspaper cuttings, are kept many medieval instruments, for example hand-carved olive-wood stamps and needles. In past times, up to 600 pilgrims were treated using a single needle.

In contrast to the technical means, the motifs have changed little over time: crosses, images of Jesus and saints or biblical scenes are just as popular as in the days of the Crusaders.

Wazzim Razzouk hopes that his son will take over the flourishing business one day. He himself tried his luck in the restaurant business as a young man. One day he chanced to see an old interview with his father Anton, who spoke with great sadness about the impending end of the family tradition. Wazzim was shocked, as his father had never criticised him or put pressure on him for this. He did not want to be responsible for such a break with history, and decided to follow in the footsteps of his forebears. It was the best decision of his life, he now says. No one who watches this passionate tattoo artist at his meticulous work will doubt the truth of his words.

Address 13 Greek Catholic Patriarchate Street, Jerusalem 97300, +972 2 5353106, www.razzouktattoo.com, www.facebook.com/RazzoukInk | Getting there Beyond the Jaffa Gate take the second street on the left to the Christian Quarter | Hours Daily 10am – 7pm | Tip The charming, comfortably old-fashioned Gloria Hotel with its bar and restaurant is the only tourist hotel (i.e. not primarily for pilgrims) within the city walls. It has a wonderful view from the roof terrace (33 Latin Patriarchate Street).

80 Rebecca Levy House

Jerusalem's first 'skyscraper'

The small Nahalat Shiva quarter was built in the second half of the 19th century. For the flood of Jewish immigrants there was hardly any space to live in the crowded Old City, so Jews bought land outside the city walls from Arabs. However, their situation in the new houses was precarious owing to attacks by Arabs. At first the new structures were used as workshops during the day, and the artisans slept in the Old City at night. Later, residential settlements with one- and two-storey houses including small courtyards were built. For security reasons, they were constructed close together around a large square, like a castle.

One well-preserved neighbourhood built to this courtyard plan is Even Yisrael in the Nachlaot district. It dates back to 1875. Here stands the rather bulky-looking building with projecting upper floors that belonged to the American millionaire Rebecca Levy and was known as The Widow's House. The people of Jerusalem saw this three-storey structure as the first 'skyscraper' in their city. Mrs Levy was thought extravagant. She married three times. Her first husband, a Mexican, died and the marriage was childless. Then she moved to Jerusalem with a Jew named Levy and bore 11 children. When husband number two died, she was an elderly woman, and married a Mexican once again, in the USA.

On this historic square, which was beautifully restored in 2004, there once stood a ritual bath, cisterns and a communal oven for baking. During the renovation work, a small amphitheatre was integrated. Nahalat Shiva is part of the urban project with the name 'Pictures in Stone'. Historic photos and information panels placed in three courtyard neighbourhoods of Nahlaot in 2008 illustrate and describe the story of the buildings. Today, many of them are still homes, but they also house small workshops, galleries and cafés.

Address Even Yisreal between Jaffa Road, Even Yisrael Street, Agrippas Street and Baruchoff Street; Rebecca Levy House: 26 King David Street, Jerusalem 9195000, +972 2 5692694 | **Getting there** Tram to Yaffo Center; bus 7, 13, 17, 19, 22, 32, 34, 71, 72, 74, 75, 77, 78, 103, 209, 211, 267 or 755 to Agrippas Street | **Tip** In the small park Gan Ha'Sus, an oasis in the city bustle, a Saturday flea market is held for jewellery, clothing, ceramics and antiques. A life-size sculpture of a black horse also stands here. The Veneti Horse of Peace by the sculptor Oskar Kogoj is a gift from Slovenia to mark the 3,000th anniversary of Jerusalem (18 King George Street).

81 La Régence

A luxurious place where the rich and powerful dine

Restaurant guides praise La Régence as one of the best in the Middle East. But the real challenge for the chefs and waiters is the unusual clientele that dines here. There is hardly any other restaurant in the region that can claim to have fed so many powerful, rich and prominent people from all over the world. Historic photos on the wood-panelled walls of the elegant room impressively testify to this.

La Régence is part of one of the world's most historic hotels, the King David, which stands majestically on a hill opposite the wall of the Old City, and offering unrivalled views. It was built in the 1930s in the Art Deco style by Jewish investors from Egypt. To this day, the fine wooden parquet floor, the exclusive furnishings, the ceiling lights and the numerous small lamps in the hotel restaurant reveal Art Deco design. The hotel quickly became luxurious accommodation for kings and presidents, the scene for historic meetings and events. These include secret talks and official peace negotiations, for example between Israel and Jordan – but also the terrorist attack by the Zionist underground organisation Irgun in 1946. It was directed against the British Mandate rulers in the building, and claimed the lives of at least 91 victims.

Traditionally, in view of the clientele, the kosher hotel cuisine and extremely well-stocked wine cellar have to meet the highest standards. Before 1949, some crowned heads of state even resided in the King David for a time after being deposed: the kings of Spain and Greece, as well as Emperor Haile Selassie of Ethiopia. Later, the hotel accommodated all presidents of the USA and German chancellors, countless other heads of state or government, and stars including Elizabeth Taylor, Richard Gere and Madonna. The restaurant serves high-class modern haute cuisine, but is also used to reacting to the special wishes of its eminent guests.

Address 23 King David Street, Jerusalem 94101, +972 2 6208795, www.danhotels.com |
Getting there Bus 4, 7, 8, 13, 18, 21, 30a, 38, 49, 71, 72, 74, 75, 101, 102, 103, 105, 106,
107 or 108 to David HaMelekh / Mapu or Yemin Moshe | Hours Sun – Thu 6.30 – 10.30pm |
Tip The large, well-kept Bloomfield Park – officially called Koret Liberty Bell Park – is right
behind the hotel. With many sculptures, fountains, sports facilities, a replica of the Liberty
Bell in the USA and small artists' colony with shops, as well as a lot of shady spots, it is a
pleasant place to linger.

82 The Rothschild House
Fascinating, not only at Hanukkah

On one of the largest and most impressive squares in the Old City, Batei Mahseh Square, stands the imposing Rothschild House with its two-storey arcaded façade. The square is at the heart of the Jewish Quarter, which took shape from the mid-19th century and today is a gem of modern architecture with historical elements. German and Dutch Jews bought land here from Arabs in order to intensify Jewish resettlement. Many Jews had already flocked to the Holy City, but most of them lived in wretched conditions in Arab wooden houses, many of which were shabby.

With the aim of helping poor families to leave the old, overcrowded districts that lacked adequate sanitary facilities, in 1871 the Frankfurt banker Baron Wilhelm Carl von Rothschild funded construction of this elegant building, in a style that is typical for Jerusalem. Like other new buildings on the square, which also came to be known as the 'German Square', the Rothschild House with its striking round arches provided considerable comfort by the standards of the time on its two floors. An unusual feature was the stone chimneys for the stoves in the house.

The Rothschild House, which became more and more dilapidated in the period when it was under Jordanian control, was renovated after the Six-Day War. Today, the building accommodates a Torah school and the offices of the organisation responsible for the reconstruction and development of the Jewish Quarter. In front of it stand the remains of a column made in the Greek style, dating from the first century before Christ. The building is especially resplendent at the time of the annual festival of lights, Hanukkah. For this event, the historic sites of the Old City are transformed into a living work of art with the aid of lighting effects. The Rothschild House participates in this festival with new video installations every year.

Address Batei Mahseh Square, Jewish Quarter, Jerusalem 9751494 | Getting there Enter the Old City through the Zion Gate | Tip About 300 metres away is the Ophel Archaeological Garden. During excavations from 1968 onwards, the ruins of buildings by various rulers over a period of 2,500 years were found in 25 strata.

83 — The Rothschild Room
Imperial splendour in the Israel Museum

After passing through a small antechamber in the Empire style, you enter the long-vanished world of feudal France. With every authentic detail, you feel you are being transported to the glittering, ostentatious Rococo period of the 18th century, an age of *joie de vivre* and (for the aristocracy) indulgence. In those days, the salon with its heavy golden chandeliers suspended from the ceiling and many candelabra, was part of the Parisian town house of a count in Rue du Bac. Specialist publications have applauded this room in the museum as 'a masterpiece of historical authenticity' – although some experts disagree with this judgement.

The style of the fanciful, delicate and opulently decorated furnishings, known as 'Louis Quinze' after King Louis XV, comes into its own when reflected in three large mirrors and seems to enlarge even further the big, sumptuously fitted salon with its gilded stucco and heavy curtains. The two Gobelin tapestries on the wall were woven specially for King Louis XV. Above the doors of the salon are allegorical depictions of the four continents, Europe, Asia, Africa and America. A marble statue and a large number of candelabra adorn the room, in which Voltaire and Madame de Pompadour would surely have felt at home.

In the late 19th century this fine residence belonged to the legendary Baron Edmond de Rothschild, who was known in the Jewish world as 'Ha-Nadiv' (the benefactor). He was a passionate supporter of Zionist ideas and invested huge sums to purchase plots of land and estates in Palestine. Rothschild encouraged Jewish settlements and started the cultivation of grapes for wine in Judaea. In 1924 he founded the Palestine Jewish Colonization Association, which bought more than 500 square kilometres of land in Palestine. Rothschild's grandchildren donated the Parisian salon to the Israel Museum in 1969.

Address 11 Derech Ruppin Boulevard, Jerusalem 9171002, +972 2 6708811 | Getting there Bus 14 or 66 to Israel Museum | Hours Sat–Mon, Wed, Thu 10am–5pm, Tue 4–7pm | Tip The Shrine of the Book is the main attraction of the Israel Museum. This impressive structure with a roof like a round tent holds originals and facsimiles of ancient scrolls of the Old Testament and other finds from Qumran on the Dead Sea.

84 Saba's Little Museum

Everyday testimony to Zionist projects

To visit this quirky museum, you have to make arrangements by telephone in advance, because its exhibition, mainly of everyday items from the Jewish settlement in Palestine in modern times, is a family project run by Debbie and Jakov Kali. Saba's Little Museum arose largely by chance. When the Kalis took over their farm in the village of Beit Meir in the mountains of Judaea from Jakov's parents more than three decades ago, as time passed they happened upon a lot of old, in some cases antique items on their land and in the surrounding area: home-made toys, furniture, agricultural equipment, books, cooking utensils and pictures, as well as the wreck of an armoured convoy vehicle from the War of Independence, a rifle from the time of Napoleon and even the remains of a 2,000-year-old olive press.

Many pieces of equipment constructed in an amateur way or apparatus that had obviously been repaired many times reflect the harsh conditions and the fight for survival of Zionist pioneers. The Kalis turned a spacious old storehouse into a museum, and many of the larger objects stand in the open air in the large garden.

This diverse collection of everyday items deriving from 100 years of history, some of them extremely weathered, can only truly be appreciated if Jakov or Debbie are invited to tell their stories about them – which they do with obvious enthusiasm. Antiquated weapons, aged radios or toasters, laboriously repaired threshing machines or sun-faded documents, banners and pictures – whatever exhibit is chosen, the amateur curators of this museum can give detailed, lively and historically well-informed accounts of its background and peculiarities. The history of the Jewish state comes to life in an unusual way.

To complement the family atmosphere of this museum, they offer their visitors tea and other drinks with home-baked cakes beneath shady trees.

Address Moshav Beit Meir 9086500, +972 54 5708592, www.machsanshelsaba.co.il | **Getting there** National route 1 towards Tel Aviv, Beit Shemesh exit, then national route 38 and after 300 metres turn into Nahal Derech Burma in the direction of Beit Meir | **Hours** By arrangement Sun–Thu 7am–9pm, Fri 7am–3pm, Sat after sunset, until 9pm | **Tip** Yitzhak Rabin Park, named after the former prime minister, has beautiful walking trails and a wonderful view of the scenery of Judaea. Excavation sites are signs of millennia-old settlements.

85__Sarah's Tent Gallery

Israeli contemporary art – critical and Zionist

The recent history of Israel is the main artistic topic in this small but significant gallery. Works by leading Israeli artists have been represented here for more than 40 years. Many of them are protagonists of 'Zionist art', which takes the Jewish state and Jewish identity as its principal theme.

Zionist art, for which a state prize has been awarded since 2010, is controversial in Israel. It extends beyond montages and paintings to include literature and cinema. Its pictures and graphic works often combine motifs from Israeli history such as the star of David, the Western Wall and the menorah with historic photographs and icons of Zionism such as Golda Meir or David Ben Gurion.

The gallery owner, Gabriel Knafo, is proud to be able to offer objects and paintings by Israel's best-known artists, for example Menashe Kadishman, Avi Bensimhon and Dan Groover, despite strong competition in Jerusalem and Tel Aviv. Many of the colourful works have a noticeable affinity to Pop Art. Some of them take the controversial debate about occupation and human rights as their subject, while others are more like a plea for heroic victory over the homelessness of the Jews across the world, which came to an end with the founding of Israel. One of the gallery's important artists is Ester Kreisman, who often works with motifs from the cityscape of Jerusalem or Tel Aviv, while David Gerstein creates colourful ceramic and aluminium sculptures.

Although Knafo has customers from all over the world, he says that collectors from the USA are still his most important clients. The prices of most images and objects are between €2,000 and €10,000. The gallery takes its name from the biblical Sarah, the wife of Abraham and founding mother of Israel. Sarah's hospitality, praised in the Old Testament, is intended to be the model for the spirit of the gallery.

Address 18 Shlomzion Hamalka, Jerusalem 94146, +972 54 4425511, www.sarahstentgallery.com | Getting there Bus 13, 19, 104, 105, 108, 115, 284, 480 or 755 to Mamilla/Agron Street | Hours Sun–Thu 10am–7pm, Fri 10am–2pm | Tip The Capricorn Bar & Karaoke is Jerusalem's first karaoke bar. Its charm consists in the colourful mix of guests from all over the world, so that many karaoke evenings are entertaining events (18 King Solomon Street, +972 2 6245415, Sun–Thu 8pm till late, Sat from 9pm).

86_ The Sephardic Deli
Proud of specialities from the shtetl

Uri and his brothers are proud of their reputation and their success on the toughest market for Israeli specialities in Jerusalem, the famous Mahane Yehuda Market. In their modest-looking corner shop there are often throngs of customers around the displays of food, with dozens of different kinds of salad, cheese and deep-fried vegetables, various sorts of marinated olives, and marinated or smoked fish fillet.

The clientele is a mirror of Israeli society. Apart from Arabs, all groups come here: an orthodox Jew with a prayer strap and a black coat, a grey-haired, bent lady, elegantly dressed as was usual in her old home in Europe, a young hipster from a start-up company, a fit-looking army officer, a young mother in a long dress with two small children clinging to it. Nowhere in Jerusalem is the diversity of society more apparent than on the bustling Mahane Yehuda Market with its 250 stalls and shops for fruit, vegetables, meat, fish, bakery products, nuts, spices, herbs and dried fruit.

When Uri's grandfather came to Jerusalem at the end of 1949, he started out with a butcher's shop, then switched to do-it-yourself products. More than 40 years ago, his sons finally fulfilled the family dream and opened a delicatessen. Although they are a Sephardic family deriving from Kurdistan, their ambition was to offer the famous specialities of the eastern European Ashkenazy Jews in addition to their oriental dishes such such as 'kubbe' (rice balls prepared in various ways) and 'zhug' (a hot spicy sauce seasoned with coriander and cumin). Customers now enthuse over their chopped chicken liver, their old-fashioned egg salad and 'gefilte fish' (literally 'stuffed' fish) – all home-made. Customers are advised to ask specifically for these delicacies, as they do not keep well, and are often left in the big refrigerated store rather than displayed in the shop for all to see.

Address Corner of 18 Mahane Yehuda Street and 2 Eshkol Street, Jerusalem 9430024, www.madany-ori.co.il, www.en.machne.co.il | **Getting there** Tram to Mahane Yehuda | **Hours** Sun–Thu 8am–6pm, Fri 8am–3pm | **Tip** The restaurant Azura in a back yard at the edge of the market is a low-cost, popular family business run by Jews of Turkish origin. They serve hearty oriental dishes such as aubergines in cinnamon sauce stuffed with minced meat and pine nuts (4 Ha-Eshkol Street, Sun–Thu 10am–4pm, Fri 10am–2pm).

87 The Shawar Bakery

A family business with a 300-year tradition

This bakery in an ancient building in the Christian Quarter is home to one of the loveliest cafés in Jerusalem, difficult to find and hardly visible from the outside. The small, cosy room for guests with comfortable, upholstered benches and large oriental cushions, small olive-wood tables and heavy, finely engraved copper trays is on the first floor of the shop, reached via a narrow staircase with a copper banister. As well as biscuits, cakes and the house pastries, there is freshly brewed Turkish and Italian coffee, various kinds of tea and freshly pressed orange or pomegranate juice.

Shawar's Bakery & Pâtisserie has been in the same family for 300 years. Its sweet specialities, such as different variations of baklava (a mixture of nuts in filo pastry), are baked in a large oven according to traditional recipes. The small, creamy pâtisserie products are also noteworthy. The prices are fairly high. In the opinion of the proprietors, the Shawar brothers, their quality and tradition justifies this. Christians come here at holy festivals such as Easter and Christmas to buy their favourite pastries, whose oriental influences are clear, however. Some items are stuffed with dates or walnuts. There are flat biscuits with sesame and honey as big as saucers, sweet loaves and painted Easter eggs. The olive oil from the family's own production is highly recommended.

For people with a sweet tooth, the Old City is a little paradise with huge variety, thanks to the different bakeries in the various quarters. The Armenian bakeries differ from the Greek ones, and the Sephardic bakeries are not the same as those in the Ashkenazy tradition. Baklava, sesame rings, 'halva' (a kind of sesame paste filled with nuts and seeds, coloured and flavoured with all sorts of extracts) and 'kanafeh' (a fine sweet cheese pastry soaked in sugar syrup) are available in a big range of varieties.

Address 54 Christian Quarter Road, Jerusalem 9761250, +972 2 6280004 | Getting there Tram to City Hall, through the Jaffa Gate, then to the right through the Armenian Quarter and left into Christian Quarter Street | Hours From morning to evening, no exact times | Tip The café in the cloister garden of St Saviour's Church is a profoundly idyllic, shady spot. The drinks and light meals are sold at normal prices, a striking contrast to almost all the places around St Saviour's and the nearby Church of the Nativity.

88__ The Shrine of Jesus
Quarrelling Christians at the holiest site

The shrine with the tomb of Jesus was splendidly restored in 2017. The aedicula, as the structure above the holiest place for Christians is known, has been freed from its steel scaffolding. Tourists and pilgrims, who often wait in long queues at the entrance to the small, dark chamber containing the tombstone and altars, now once again have access to the building at the heart of the Church of the Holy Sepulchre following its expensive restoration. This is hardly to the credit of the six churches represented in this complex edifice with its numerous chapels and altars: the clergy have been profoundly at odds with each other for centuries.

This also applied to the issue of restoration. The guardians of the sanctuary, the Greek and Armenian Orthodox churches as well as the Copts and Catholics, could not even agree on who was allowed to remove the remains of candles or sweep the steps. In view of the dangerously crumbling condition of the aedicula, the Israeli heritage authorities gave the churches no option: they threatened to close the church as it was a danger to life and limb. Back in 1947 the British authorities took the same course. There is a tradition of foreign rule in the Church of the Holy Sepulchre. Since Ottoman times, two Muslim families have been in charge of the building and its keys. Questions about rights in the church are decided by the *status quo* laid down 160 years ago by the sultan.

The complex building works in the church carried out under Greek leadership are a blessing for the 1.5 million annual visitors. The paintings of the resurrection of Christ on the walls and ceiling have been cleaned and are plain to see again. A new window gives a view of the ancient rock tomb below. Archaeologists were disappointed, however, not to be involved in the work or in the first opening of the tomb slab for almost 200 years. The churches insisted on this.

Address Sukh el-Dabbagha, Jerusalem 9114002 | **Getting there** Tram to City Hall, then to the Jaffa Gate and along David Street and Christian Quarter Street to the Sukh el-Dabbagha | **Hours** The Muslim key-holders open up at sunrise and close at sunset | **Tip** Zalatimo, a small café a little hidden away round the corner, has been run by the Zalatimo family for 200 years. Their speciality is mutabak, made from filo pastry, with a delicate aroma of spices, filled with nuts or cheese. One wall of the café is said to date from Herod's time.

89__The Shtetl

A trip back in time in Mea Shearim

To come to Mea Shearim, the realm of the orthodox Jews, is to feel you have been transported into the lost world of the shtetl, the villages and quarters of the Ashkenazy Jews of eastern Europe. Especially on the Shabbat, when traffic, never dense at any time, is strictly banned, an anachronistic tranquillity dominates the narrow alleys with their low buildings, in which there are neither televisions nor radios.

You only hear voices. In the back yards, on the square and little streets, countless dark-clad boys with sidelocks and girls wearing dresses down to their ankles are at play. The district appears uncared-for, shabby and down-at-heel in many places. On balconies and verandas washing is hung out and junk is piled up. Synagogues, grubby shops selling all kinds of things, old-fashioned artisan workshops, stores crammed full of Judaica and jewellery set the scene. On the walls of the buildings are posters for information and agitation, as well as mouldy money-collecting tins belonging to Hassidic groups that are often in conflict with each other. All of this conveys the message that higher values matter more here than external appearances on the street.

Mea Shearim was designed in 1846 by the German Protestant architect and missionary Conrad Schick to give pious Jews an alternative to the overcrowded Old City. By 1900 about 300 houses, a flour mill and a bakery had been built here. To this day, Yiddish or English is spoken here. For orthodox Jews, who call themselves 'Haredin' (those who tremble before God), Hebrew is reserved for prayer and the scriptures.

Among the orthodox groups there are traditionally strict opponents of Zionism who reject a secular Israel as blasphemous. Organisations such as Neturei Karta therefore demonstrate against Israel along with anti-Semites and radical Palestinians, not only in Europe but also often in Mea Shearim.

Address Entrance from many sides, for example the corner of Shlomo Zalman Baharan Street and HaRav Shmuel Salant Street | **Getting there** Tram to City Hall or Jaffa Center; bus 1, 22 or 34 to Straus / Prague | **Hours** It is advisable not to go to Mea Shearim on the Shabbat, to be decently dressed and never in a large group, as the residents do not want to be examined as if they were in a museum. The orthodox sometimes react drastically to what they regard as interlopers showing no respect. | **Tip** The Olive Wood Factory is an old-established shop selling its own products: Judaica, but also many everyday items and personalised door signs at relatively moderate prices (26 Mea Shearim Street).

90 The Siebenberg House

A private museum with ancient treasures

The story of the Siebenberg House is material for a novel. An ambitious young man and his remarkable wife want to fulfil a grand dream, spend a fortune on it, are met with scorn and hostility for years on account of their stubbornness, and have to overcome the resistance of scholars, bureaucrats and jealous opponents – finally discovering a treasure and making a chapter in the history of Jerusalem. But this is not fiction – it really happened.

Theo Siebenberg came from an old family of diamond dealers in Antwerp. He made a fortune as a businessman and married Miriam, a young artist. Together they dreamed of making a life in Jerusalem. When Israel gained complete control of the city in 1967, they bought a plot of land in the ruined, war-torn district near the Temple Mount. They invested a lot of money in their new building in the quickly growing Jewish Quarter, which was getting a new look through strict planning controls, a lot of historical awareness, enormous sums of money and the arrival of many orthodox Jews. Everywhere in this district, archaeologists were looking for traces of the past, and Siebenberg believed that ancient artefacts lay beneath his house. However, the experts disputed this and the neighbours were worried about the stability of their foundations. Disputes and court cases began and lasted for years.

In the end, the amateur archaeologist Siebenberg emerged victorious. The ground beneath his house proved to be an archaeological gold mine, and specialists paid tribute to him. The result is a museum, opened in 1985 and continually extended, in the maze of alleys of the clean and tidy Jewish Quarter. Visitors see excavations and 100 finds, some more than 2,000 years old: arrowheads, jewellery, keys, glass, ceramics and coins. At depths of up to 18 metres, a mikvah (Jewish ritual bath), an aqueduct, a Byzantine cistern and royal tombs were discovered.

Address 5 Beit-Ha'shoeva Street, Jerusalem 9751722, +972 2 6282341 or
+972 54 7267754, www.siebenberghouse.com | Getting there Enter the Old City
through the Zion Gate | Hours By arrangement | Tip The Zion Gate was built in
1540 by Suleiman the Magnificent with a hole above the archway for pouring boiling
oil on attackers. The gate was also built with a right-angle turn to prevent riders
from charging through.

91 The Slave's Palace
Mamluk architecture for a refugee

The pale beige striped façades, the layered stalactite vault and the artistic gate niches of some of the buildings convey an impression of the splendour of Mamluk rule in the Holy City. The former Serai es-Sitt Tunshuq palace, a place shrouded in secrecy in Aqabat-at-Takiya Street, is not in good condition, however. According to tradition it was built for Princess Tunshuq, known as the Mistress of Alms and Benefactions, in 1388 during her years of exile in Jerusalem. She was not a true-born princess, but a former slave who is said to have fled here from Turkey or Mongolia. The somewhat dilapidated house with three gates in which this woman lived for 11 years, is now used as an orphanage for Arab boys. Before her death in 1399, Tunshuq ordered the construction of a mausoleum directly opposite the palace. Her tomb is inside it behind the two barred windows.

Traces of the Mamluk period can be found scattered here and there in the southern part of the Muslim Old City. Usually they can be recognised by the austere dark and light stripes on the façades. The Mamluks came from Egypt. They were descended from warrior slaves, and came to be rulers in the Holy Land in the 13th century during conflicts with Crusaders and Mongol tribes. After conquering the last bastion of the Crusaders in Accon in 1291 and driving the Mongols from Syria, they ruled large areas of the region for about two centuries.

In Palestine, the number of Christians was diminishing, while churches and Christian buildings fell into decay. In Jerusalem, the Mamluks built Koranic schools and hostels for pilgrims, usually of smooth masonry in red, white and black. Today these buildings are in use as homes, so visitors can only occasionally look inside the houses or into a courtyard through an open gate. The best opportunity for admiring Mamluk architecture is to look at the Ribat Mansuri hostel for pilgrims.

Address Aqabat-at-Takiya Street, Jerusalem 91140 | Getting there Tram to the
Damascus Gate, then along Beit HaBad Street and left into Aqabat-at-Takiya Street |
Tip The Sebil Bab An-Nazir fountain, dating from 1537, is one of seven that the
Ottomans built in the Old City. It has twisted columns and is opulently adorned with
rosettes and garlands (Alaa Ad Din Street, at the end of Aqabat-at-Takiya Street).

92__The Smiling House
A sundial for the orthodox

The sundial with a five-metre diameter on its façade seems to turn the narrow building on busy Jaffa Road into a smiley. But this peculiarity is not some stylistic signature by the architect – it has a practical function. For a century, the clocks and dial on the Zoharei Chama (literally 'sunrise') Synagogue have provided precise orientation for orthodox local residents and shown them when day breaks, especially the holy day, the Shabbat.

For Jews, the day begins and ends at the moment, constantly changing, of sunrise and sunset. Today, the exact times of these events, important moments for Jews as the time, for example, for morning prayer, are communicated in the media. Before the sundial was installed in Jerusalem, the orthodox had to climb to the summit of the Mount of Olives or the hills of the Bayit Vegan district every morning and evening in order to determine the precise position of the sun.

The three-storey stone building with its added wooden attic is clearly marked by wind and weather, and by a fire that broke out in 1941, despite having been restored in 1980. The synagogue, which has a 'Shabbat siren' on the roof to signal the start of the holy day, is one of the few surviving buildings constructed in the early days of the Jewish resettlement of Palestine.

Above the entrance, a plaque dating from 1908 commemorates Rabbi Shmuel Levy, who set up a lottery in his old homeland, the USA, and raised donations from philanthropists to finance his 'Great House of Teaching' in Jerusalem. The purpose of the project was to help Jewish immigrants. The upper floor became the Zoharei Chama Synagogue, while the lower storeys were a hostel that could accommodate up to 50 guests. Only a few years ago, the somewhat ramshackle building was used as a shelter for people in need and a soup kitchen. Now it is just a house of prayer – but for men only.

Address 92 Jaffa Road, Jerusalem 9434127, www.facebook.com/pages/Zoharei Chama Synagogue | **Getting there** Tram, bus 9, 18, 25, 32, 45, 74, 75 or 78 to Mahane Yehuda | **Tip** Nearby Trattoria Haba has a great variety of bread, traditional Jewish baked goods such as challah and strudel, and excellent light meals, desserts and break-fasts. There are tables inside and outside (119 Jaffa Road, +972 2 6233379, Sun – Thu 7am – 11pm, Fri 7am – 2pm).

93 — Synagogues From Around the World

Displaying Judaism in the Israel Museum

Four synagogues, from Surinam, India, Germany and Italy, authentically re-erected in the Israel Museum, demonstrate the cultural variety of Judaism. The airy Tzedek ve-Shalom Synagogue from Surinam, with its plain decoration, makes Jewish life in the tropics tangible. This neoclassically influenced, brightly lit synagogue with a gallery around the walls and a white wooden balustrade, simple wooden benches and a gilded chandelier once stood on sand in Paramaribo. It was built in 1736 by emigrants to what was then the capital of Dutch Guyana. The Jewish settlers came from Spain and Portugal, but had fled to Holland in fear of the Inquisition.

The oldest of the four, the Kadavumbagam Synagogue from the Indian city of Cochin, dates from the 16th century. Richly adorned with wood carvings, it was constructed over the ruins of an even older synagogue. The Jewish congregation in Cochin is said to be 2,000 years old, but most of its members emigrated in the 1950s. Many of the carvings, the Torah ark and the lectern betray the influence of the decorations on Indian Hindu temples. As was usual in India, the floor of the synagogue was covered in carpets or mats on which worshippers walked barefoot.

The synagogue of Horb, a small town near Bamberg in Germany, has impressive wall and ceiling paintings, but they are weathered and damaged in places. With its vaulted ceiling, the synagogue was built on the upper floor of a half-timbered building in the 18th century. This structure was later converted into a barn, and the paintings were not rediscovered until 1908. The Italian synagogue with its gilding dates from the 18th century and came from Vittorio Veneto near Venice. It has a gallery for women, strictly partitioned off and barred.

Address 11 Derech Ruppin Boulevard, Jerusalem 9171002, +972 2 6708811 | Getting there Bus 14 or 66 to Israel Museum | Hours Sun, Mon, Wed, Thu 10am–5pm, Tue 4–9pm, Fri 10am–2pm, Sat 10.30am–4pm | Tip The exhibition of modern Israeli art in the Edmond and Lily Safra Wing of the Israel Museum includes works by the leading exponents of contemporary art since 1949, for example Menashe Kadishman and Reuven Rubin. As well as paintings and drawings, sculptures and other objects are also on view.

94__ Te'enim

A hidden oasis with a stunning view

For a moment, a guest might think that this high-class, stylishly furnished vegetarian restaurant with its young clientele is somewhere in Berlin or San Francisco. But a glance through the large windows to the sublime walls of the Old City and David's City, illuminated at night, suffices to realise that it is one of a kind. Te'enim, tucked away in a garden on a hillside below the King David Hotel, is a little oasis of peace and quiet. It is one of the favoured places to eat for some well-known writers and scientists, who often come to sit here with their papers or laptops at the tables with ceramic tiles. There are also some seats on the small, cosy terrace in the shade of olive trees.

This restaurant in the picturesque Yemin Moshe district has an ambitious menu with European-Asian-Middle Eastern cross-over creations. The French chef Patrick Melki also serves traditional Jewish dishes such as the famous 'Jerusalem ball' (a spicy pasta bake, cooked for hours) or sweet 'blintzes' (delicious pancakes stuffed with cream cheese) and popular vegetarian dishes made with tofu or quinoa. Vegans can select from the specials, which change daily, and other meals such as grilled tofu, 'mejadara' (a dish of rice, lentils and onions) or the subtly flavoured aubergine dip 'baba ganoush'.

The Israeli wines are organically grown, and the staff also take great trouble in preparing the numerous kinds of tea and coffee, as well as freshly squeezed juices. Te'enim (which means 'figs') numbers several of Israel's top chefs among its customers, including the German-born cook Tom Franz. Located on the premises of Confederation House, it is just one of many vegan or vegetarian restaurants in Jerusalem. Israel has a reputation as a global centre for meat-free cuisine. There are said to be more vegetarian and vegan eateries in the country than anywhere else in the world.

Address 12 Emil Bote, Jerusalem 9107102, +972 2 6251967, www.teenim.rest.co.il |
Getting there Bus 13, 18, 30a or 49 to David HaMelekh / Mapu or Yemin Moshe |
Hours Sun–Thu 10am–10pm, Fri 10am–1.30pm | Tip The Kalman Sultanik
Confederation House, to which Te'enim belongs, is an arts centre for ethnic music and
poetry in a historic building. There is a varied programme of music and poetry, and
several festivals each year, for example the International Oud Festival for Arab music
(12 Emil Bote, Jerusalem 9107102, +972 2 6245206, www.confederationhouse.org/en).

95 The Temple Institute

Research for dangerous visions

In this institute, which claims to be scholarly, a lot of dreams are dreamed. Some think these dreams are highly dangerous. The orthodox Jews who have established an impressive museum in the Old City are motivated by the vision of rebuilding the Jewish temple. The first, Solomon's Temple, was destroyed by the Babylonians in the 6th century BCE, the second in 70 CE by the Romans. The Temple Institute wants to prepare the ground for the 'Third Temple' by means of research and educational work.

However, the desired site for it, the Temple Mount, is under Islamic control today. The Dome of the Rock and the Al Aqsa Mosque stand here. Only parts of the retaining wall of the Temple Mount, the Western Wall, remain in Jewish hands. The founders of the Temple Institute wish to change this. They believe that the ruins of the historic Jewish temple lie beneath the Islamic sites. There is some evidence for this, but a Jewish claim to the Temple Mount has enormously incendiary political consequences. At the Temple Institute, paintings of the Temple Mount on which the Muslim holy sites have disappeared, have been hung on the walls.

In the museum of the institute is an elaborate, scale model of the Second Temple made from marble, gold and copper, as well as several originals and replicas of vessels, musical instruments and fabrics from the age of Herod. The robes of Jewish high priests, adorned with gems, are on display in glass cases, along with copies of temple utensils for religious rituals. Some people say that all of these items have been produced in readiness for the day when there will be a new temple on Temple Mount. Moreover, the institute has also founded a school for descendants of the Levi tribe, who traditionally are the source of priests. The pupils of this school are to be prepared to resume their service in the 'Third Temple'.

Address 19 Misgav Ladach Street, Jerusalem 9751537, +972 2 6708811,
www.templeinstitute.org | Getting there Enter the Jewish Quarter via the Jaffa Gate
or Damascus Gate | Hours Sun–Thu 9am–5pm, Fri 9am–noon | Tip Hurva Square is
a large space with cafés, restaurants, a few shops and the Hurva Synagogue, and above
all a meeting point for residents of the Jewish Quarter. On the Shabbat, orthodox Jews
honour their holy day by wearing their best clothes.

96 _ Tmol Shilshom

A favourite café for literature and blind dates

Israel's writers love this café in a narrow street in the Nachalat Shiva district. With its nooks and books, stylish dining tables, old settees and armchairs, bookcases and niches, it has become a literary institution in Jerusalem. Authors such as David Grossmann, Eva Illouz, A. B. Yehoshua, Etgar Keret and Amos Oz have presented their latest works here.

David Ehrlich, the owner of the café, is a creative writer himself, who even made his own café the setting for one of his plays. He also edited the *Book of Love* in Tmol Shilshom, a portrait in words and pictures of couples who found happiness in the café – often at a blind date, as Tmol Shilshom is a place where people come to meet for the first time. Not only lovers of literature appreciate this 19th-century building with its slightly old-fashioned romantic atmosphere and its small courtyard.

When Ehrlich, who also worked as a journalist, returned from the USA after a few years, he dreamed of opening a book café, of which there are many in America. But since 1994, when Tmol Shilshom opened with a reading by the poet Yehuda Amichai, it has developed in its very own way. It has almost become a second home for some poets, writers and academics from the university; it also became the scene of passionate discussions about politics and literature, especially during the Jerusalem authors' festival and the book fair. Many of the events are held in English.

The café has meanwhile gained a reputation in some circles as a gastronomic centre. The opportunity to read or buy books here has become less important. Instead, many customers come to enjoy the skilfully prepared dishes, which are mainly vegetarian. The most popular items on the menu are the deep-fried quinoa balls with tahini sauce, the salad with roast beetroot and the spicy dish of eggs, peppers, onions and tomatoes known as 'shakshuka'.

Address 5 Yo'el Moshe Salomon, Jerusalem 9463305, +972 2 6232758, www.tmolshilshom.co.il/en | **Getting there** Tram to Jaffa Center or City Hall | **Hours** Sun–Thu 8.30am–11pm, Fri 8.30am until one hour before sunset, Sat one hour after sunset until midnight | **Tip** Zion Square, the central square in West Jerusalem, is a magnet for buskers, acrobats, dance groups, religious activists and young people, as well as a venue for demonstrations and protests. In summer a piano stands here for anyone to play.

97 — The Tongues

A horror slide on a children's playground

The frightening monster slide stands on a children's playground in small, quiet Rabinovich Park in the Kiryat Yovel district. When she made it in 1972, it was clear to the French artist Niki de Saint Phalle that the three-tongued slide might terrify children – and in the same way the local residents reacted with alarm when this enormous, colourful piece of play equipment, made from concrete and metal, was first installed.

The artist argued, referring to the psychologist Bruno Bettelheim, that the threatening face of the Mifletzet on a safe place for playing could help children to conquer their fears and overcome them. This point of view has not really been put into practice on other playgrounds around the world, but in Jerusalem, a city that has known suffering, been fought over and often endangered, Niki de Saint Phalle's argument fell on fertile soil. It certainly also helped that the mayor at that time, the legendary Teddy Kollek, was delighted by the horror slide.

The black-and-white monster's face with three tongues (accessed by staircases) serving as slides was supposed to have been called *The Golem*. The Golem is a mysterious figure in Jewish literature and kabbalistic mysticism, a human-like, silent giant of clay. However, the popular name *Mifletzet* (*The Monster*) soon gained acceptance.

With this work the artist, according to her own words, wanted to counter the image of the weak woman. The slide represents a strong woman, she says, who is devouring the park but at the same time communicating a positive mood. The children who slide out of the cave-like darkness of the head into the light are symbolising the process of birth. In 2009, it was threatened as it no longer met new technical regulations for safety on children's playgrounds. It was saved by being declared no longer merely an installation for playing but an irreplaceable work of art.

Address Corner of Tahone Street and Chile Street, Kiryat Hayovel, Jerusalem 9670102 |
Getting there Bus 23 to Chile / Korzcak; bus 19 or 33 to HaMifletset / Tahon | Tip
On the playground of the zoo two kilometres away are further works by this artist:
23 colourful mosaic sculptures of the animals of Noah's Ark, a gift to Kollek for his
90th birthday in 2002 (1 Derech Aharon Shulov, Sun–Thu 9am–7pm, Fri 9am–4.30pm,
Sat 10am–6pm).

98 The Trappist Monastery
Culture and delicacies at a place of fighting

The Latrun Monastery, a refuge of Trappist monks occupying a pretty spot on a hillside in the Ayalon Valley, is not only a religious site and a place of tranquillity. It is also a flourishing agricultural estate that produces liqueurs, fruit juice, honey, olives, oil and herbs, as well as highly acclaimed wines, and sells them in the monastery shop.

The historical renown of Latrun, on the margins of the Judaean uplands, is based on a lot of fighting and battles, however. Back in biblical times there were conflicts here between Jews and Canaanites, Maccabees and Seleucids, and later between Mamluks and Crusaders. In 1890, French monks built a monastery on a 200-hectare site. In World War I they were driven out by the Ottomans, returned in 1919, and from 1927 built the monastery and church with elements of the Byzantine and Gothic styles.

In the course of decades about two dozen Trappists, who have taken a vow of silence because of 'the sanctity of the word' and very seldom speak, have created well-tended gardens and orchards, olive groves and vineyards on the hilly terrain. Recently, the monastery has begun to hold concerts, farmers' markets and events for children.

In modern times, too, this idyllic place on the West Bank has seen bloody fighting, as it has a strategically important location between Jerusalem and Tel Aviv. In the War of Independence in 1948, the Israelis tried and failed several times to take positions held by Arab forces, and suffered heavy losses in doing so. Not until the Six-Day War was Israel able to occupy the Jordanian-controlled police station.

The name 'Latrun' is thought to derive from the 12th-century Crusader castle La Tour des Chevaliers, though some believe the name has an Arabic origin, or that it is connected with the Latin word 'latro' (thief) and was the home of the 'repentant thief' who was crucified next to Jesus.

Address Latrun Interchange, Ramla 7210701, +972 8 9255180, www.latroun.net/fr/
accueil | Getting there From Jerusalem and Tel Aviv take national route 1, exit at Latrun |
Hours Monastery (some parts) and church: summer, Mon–Sat 8.30am–noon &
3.30–5pm; winter, Mon–Sat 8.30–11am & 2.30–4pm; monastery shop 7.30am–6pm |
Tip The ruins of the castle Toron des Chevaliers, which was razed in 1244 by the Mamluks,
date from the 12th century and are well worth seeing. Since 1973 an ecumenical meeting
place for Christians in Israel has been here.

99__ The Tunnel of Judaism
A mysterious passage beneath the Western Wall

A walk through this tunnel deep under the Western Wall (Wailing Wall) leaves few people unmoved. The cramped conditions in the narrow, dimly lit passages, the massive, thick walls, the enigmatic niche and the knowledge that even the simplest questions remain unanswered in this historic place – these things make groups of visitors unusually quiet. And no one is allowed to come here alone.

Many traces of the age of the Second Temple and later eras can be identified in the tunnel. Moreover, here you see more of the Western Wall than in the entire publicly accessible overground part of the Jewish holy site, which is 60 metres long above ground, The underground part of the tunnel runs the whole length of the Western Wall, a total of about 480 metres. To this day, most of the wall has not been uncovered.

It remains unclear how, in the year 19 BCE, King Herod's architects succeeded in transporting stones of enormous size to build the temple and place them in the retaining walls. In the tunnel you can see the biggest stone in the Western Wall, called the 'Wailing Stone'. It is almost 14 metres long, 3 metres high and several metres thick, weighing an estimated 500 tonnes. It is thought to be the heaviest thing that was ever moved by humans without the aid of modern equipment. When the Romans destroyed the temple some 90 years later, only parts of the retaining wall were preserved.

The first excavations were carried out by British researchers in the 19th century. As soon as the Israelis had taken control of the whole of Jerusalem after the Six-Day War in 1967, they made great efforts to intensify the archaeological work. In the tunnel is the place that Jews believe is closest to the holy of holies in the temple. This small, separate space is today a synagogue, 'The Cave', and was where the early Muslims permitted the Jews to pray, close to the temple ruins.

Address The 75-minute tunnel tour starts on the north side of the Western Wall and ends in the Via Dolorosa, +972 2 6271333, www.english.thekotel.org/western_wall_sites | Getting there From the Damascus Gate along the Via Dolorosa to the Muslim Quarter, then towards the Temple Mount; the Western Wall is signposted | Hours Tours: Sun–Thu 7.20am until late in the evening, Fri 7.20am–noon | Tip In the Sharsheret Ha Dorot (Chain of Generations) museum next to the tunnel entrance, artefacts from 4,000 years of Jewish history, a multimedia show and nine glass sculptures by Jeremy Langford are on display (Sun–Thu 8am until the evening, Fri 9am–noon).

100__ The Tzuba Vineyard

A living kibbutz thanks to ambitious managers

In modern Israel, kibbutzim have lost their significance as one of the great visions of the Jewish state. Young people are less and less enthusiastic about the idea of a cooperative run on egalitarian, democratic lines whose members all have equal rights. Just less than two per cent of Israelis live in a kibbutz today, whereas the figure was once eight per cent. Those who have survived are mainly the ones who had business success and where private property and raising children in the family instead of a children's home are permitted. One of these kibbutzim is Tzuba, south of Jerusalem. It owes its success to the flourishing vineyard.

This kibbutz put its faith in modern management and innovative ideas from an early stage. Factories making bullet-proof glass and chocolate reduce the traditional dependence on olives, fruit and vegetables. In addition, a comfortable hotel with 64 suites and a leisure park were opened here, at an altitude of 700 metres in the lovely mountain scenery of Judaea. In 1996 the son of a winemaker, Paul Dubbs, who had emigrated from South Africa, was looking for a challenge in Israel. He found it in establishing the Tzuba vineyard, a task that took almost 10 years. Various kinds of grape were cultivated, oak barrels were imported from France, cork from Portugal, technical equipment from Germany and other countries. One of the secrets of the Israeli wine industry, which now earns great acclaim and has been expanding rapidly since the 1980s, lies in its aim of employing the best materials from around the globe and wine experts from all over the world.

The most successful of them is the 'boutique' vineyard Tzuba, with an annual production of 30,000 bottles and a Chardonnay that has won several international prizes. Merlot, Shiraz and Sangiovese grapes are also grown, and dessert wines using Cabernet Sauvignon and Chardonnay are made.

Address Kibbutz Tzuba 90870, +972 2 5347678, www.tzubawinery.co.il | Getting there Superbus 183 from Binyanei Aouma in Jerusalem; by road national route 1 from Jerusalem towards Tel Aviv, exit to Mevasseret Tzion, then turn left and drive 4 kilometres to the Sataf Circle roundabout, turn right on to road no. 395, then 2 kilometres to Tzuba | Hours Sun–Thu 10am–4pm, Fri 10am–2pm, also by arrangement; book wine tastings and tours from Tzuba Tourism, +972 2 5347000 | Tip Israel Wine Journeys in Jerusalem runs trips to many vineyards (7 Diskin Street, Sun–Thu 8am–7pm, Fri 8am–3pm, +972 54 3136908, www.israelwinejourneys.net).

101__ The Underground Prisoners Museum

It's all authentic – even the escape tunnel

The low-ceilinged, windowless executioner's room with the gallows and the trapdoor in the wooden floor has lost none of its frightening, dark atmosphere. Next to it are the bare death cells in which condemned prisoners awaited execution. Today, the former British central gaol, which was mainly used for holding Zionist underground fighters, is a museum. However, those who were executed here were mainly Arab prisoners. The rulers of the British Mandate sent Jews who had been condemned to death to a prison in Akko so that they would not have to execute them in the Holy City.

The Underground Prisoners Museum seems as if it had been abandoned only yesterday. Thanks to a great love of detail and the authenticity of the rooms, equipment and furnishings, visitors gain an extremely life-like impression of the brutal mood in the years when the Zionist fighters of Haganah, Irgun and Lehi paved the way for the establishment of the Jewish state. Before the rulers of the British Mandate for Palestine converted the building on the Russian estate in Jerusalem into a prison, it was used as a hostel for pilgrims and Russian women. After the British drove the Turks from Jerusalem in 1917, they made the extensive site with its large courtyard into a central prison. In the late 1940s, the people behind bars here were principally Zionist politicians, activists and members of paramilitary Jewish organisations.

Even the precisely fitted-out room of the prison governor creates the impression that at any moment a British officer might take a seat behind the massive desk with its old-fashioned army telephone. The sanatorium, the bakery, the library and the guard rooms have been recreated with equal authenticity. And it is even possible for visitors to see one of the escape tunnels dug by the inmates.

Address 1 Rehov Mishol Hagvura, Jerusalem 9131401, +972 2 6233166 | **Getting there** Tram to City Hall; bus 1, 6, 6a, 17, 19 or 66 to HaIriyah LRT | **Hours** Sun–Thu 9am–5pm, Fri 10am–1pm | **Tip** The monumental Russian Orthodox Church of the Holy Trinity is one block away. Built in 1870, the church with four massive, octagonal towers and green domes is considered a masterpiece of Russian religious architecture. With its precious icons it is visited today by Russian pilgrims (Moskva Square, Mon–Fri 9am–1pm).

102__ The Valley of Zurim

Where tourists assist archaeologists

As a rule, archaeologists fear the activities of amateurs, who can un-wittingly destroy valuable objects or evidence. This makes it all the more remarkable that in Jerusalem the opportunity to help experts in their excavations is offered to tourists. In a large tent in the Valley of Zurim, under instruction from archaeologists and their assistants, they can search in the area around the Temple Mount for artefacts that are thousands of years old. This involves digging through huge piles of earth that the WAQF, the Islamic administration authority, heaped up in the Kidron Valley. Responsible for the Temple Mount, the WAQF dumped huge quantities of rubble and building waste – about 300 truckloads – from terrain that is historically highly inter-esting, the so-called 'Stables of Solomon' at the south-eastern corner of the Temple Mount.

Israeli experts took over the care of this rubble and included their laborious investigations in an archaeological education project for examining the antiquities on the Temple Mount. In the pretty Emek Tzurim National Park at the foot of the Mount of Olives, following a short archaeological briefing, participants can sift carefully through rubble from buildings, or assist experts in sorting the finds.

The value of this project, supported by the Israeli authority for an-tiquities, is shown by thousands of objects, included shards of ancient vases, tiles and bowls, coins from Herod's time and later, arrowheads and crucifixes from the Crusader period and mosaic stones from the age of the Mamluks. Participants in the projects are given a certifi-cate as a keepsake from their archaeological adventure. Since 2005, almost 200,000 volunteers have taken part in the project, which is controversial in Israel. Some scholars criticise that the finds are be-ing retrieved from a rubbish dump and cannot be assigned exactly to a place of origin.

Address Emek Tzurim National Park, Derech Har Hatsofim, Jerusalem 91196, +972 2 5667067, www.tmsifting.org | **Getting there** Bus 48 or 84 to Beit Orot/Lempel | **Hours** To join in, contact the information centre in the Valley of Zurim | **Tip** The Russian Orthodox Church of Mary Magdalen with its gilded onion domes and blue roofs is the most striking building on the Mount of Olives. It was built in 1885 by Tsar Alexander III to honour his mother, Tsarina Maria Alexandrovna.

103 The Venetian Synagogue
Israel's finest Jewish temple?

It is regarded as the most beautiful synagogue in Israel, yet is used regularly only by the small congregation of Italian Jews in Jerusalem. The wood-panelled prayer room with its magnificent Torah ark, fine ceiling paintings and sumptuous chandeliers once stood in the small Italian town of Conegliano, between Venice and Padua, where Jews lived from the 16th century. As hardly any Jews remained there in the early 20th century, the Rococo synagogue dating from the early 18th century, including some elements that were even older, was in danger of decaying.

When a military rabbi from the Austro-Hungarian army, which was occupying northern Italy, chanced upon the synagogue in 1918, it had long been closed up. Rabbi Harry Deutsch was desperately seeking a place for Jewish soldiers to pray at the Jewish New Year when he discovered the disused synagogue. Some 33 years later, Deutsch was present when the building, which had been transported piece by piece to Israel, was ceremoniously reopened in Jerusalem.

The Italian Jewish community in Jerusalem holds its prayers here according to the traditional 'Rome ritual', which is more than 2,000 years old and is among the oldest surviving Jewish rituals. Today, the synagogue is part of the Umberto Nahon Museum of Italian Jewish Art with its research centre for Jewish culture in Italy.

A large number of superbly adorned scriptures on paper and parchment from the history of the Jews in Italy, embroidered velvet and damask fabrics, precious carvings and valuable Hanukka lamps can be seen in the museum. Among the highlights are 300-year-old, richly decorated and beautifully written ketubahs (Jewish marriage contracts), medieval ritual artefacts and elaborate circumcision chairs with fine upholstery and carvings, as well as Baroque and Renaissance furniture. The oldest object is wood panelling in the Torah ark dating from 1450.

Address 27 Hillel Street, Jerusalem 9195000, +972 2 6241610, www.ijamuseum.org |
Getting there Tram to Yaffo Center; bus 7, 13, 19, 22 or 77 to King George Street |
Hours Sun, Tue & Wed 10.30am–4.30pm, Mon noon–7pm, Fri 10am–1pm | **Tip**
The Friends of Zion, a museum 200 metres away, is a multimedia presentation of the
support that Israel and the Jews have received from non-Jews. In 2018, the museum
awarded a prize to President Donald Trump for his policy on Israel (20 Yosef Rivlin
Street, Sun–Thu 9.30am–6pm, Fri 9.30am–2pm, Sat 10am–6pm, +972 2 5329400).

104_ Vic's Art Studio

Armenian ceramics for presidents and stars

Vic Lepejian is an institution in Jerusalem. Not only the Armenian patriarch of Jerusalem, who lives just round the corner, gives him commissions, such as the large memorial mosaic to mark the 100th anniversary of the genocide committed against Armenians. Works by the ceramic artist Lepejian can also be found in many other churches and monasteries in the Old City, as well as in municipal buildings, and in residences and hotels in the Muslim eastern sector of the city. Israeli ministries order gifts for guests of state from his small basement shop. One of the recipients was the former American president Barack Obama, who according to Lepejian was presented with an unusual ceramic mosaic displaying motifs of Jerusalem, with several breaks in its design.

Lepejian is one of many Armenian craftsmen in Jerusalem who – in a line going back several generations – make hand-painted, twice-fired ceramic objects in a strictly traditional way: tiles, portraits, mosaics, large images and decorations. It is true that almost every souvenir shop in Israel sells hundreds of ceramic items. However, most of them are mass-produced, something that is difficult for most people to recognise. At Vic's Armenian Art Studio, every single individual piece has been painted by hand, the owner promises. He opened his shop when still a young man in 1975 and was soon successful. Since then his works have been shown at exhibitions in many countries.

Having been trained at the Armenian State Academy of Fine Arts in Erivan, Lepejian feels as committed as ever to strict standards of craftsmanship. He is the winner of many awards, and over the years has cultivated modern influences in ceramic art. He likes to employ unusual or abstract motifs, to break up smooth surfaces, to work in plain black-and-white, or with gaudy colours, and he is continually in search of new perspectives.

Address 77 Armenian Patriarchate Road, Jerusalem 9191141, +972 2 6280496,
www.viclepejian.mysite.com | Getting there Tram to City Hall, then from the Jaffa
Gate the first street on the right into the Old City, or bus 1, 3, 38, 104, 117, 234 or
480 to Jaffa Gate | Hours Mon–Sat 9am–7pm | Tip Bulghourji is a restaurant serving
traditional Armenian dishes a few metres from Vic's shop (6 Armenian Patriarchate
Street, +972 53 9443920).

105 __ The Viennese Oasis
Coffee-house heaven in the Austrian hostel

If you take a Friday stroll from the Damascus Gate to the Old City, in narrow El Wad Street you are inevitably caught up in a slow-moving flow of thousands of Muslims on their way to the Temple Mount. Tourists who stray here get a friendly reception, but after a few hundred metres more in the dense crowd, they will feel relieved to open the wooden door of the Austrian Hospice at the third corner and find a seemingly different universe beyond it.

In this weighty building is a well-kept idyll with the charm of the old Danube monarchy. At the reception desk stands an old Austrian post box, on the wall hangs a large portrait of Emperor Franz Joseph, who stayed here in 1869. In the Wiener Kaffeehaus (Viennese Coffee House) you feel at the heart of old Europe: chandeliers on vaulted ceilings, benches and chairs of dark wood, upholstered with red fabric, gold-framed mirrors and old-fashioned pictures. Here you don't just order coffee, but a 'Kleiner Brauner' (mocha with a jug of milk) or a 'Fiaker' (with sugar, Schnapps and cream). 'Vienna Schnitzel' and 'Sacher Torte' are on the menu.

Viennese atmosphere continues in the pretty green garden. The small metal bistro tables are scattered beneath shady palms and cypresses. On the roof terrace where the Austrian flag flutters, you have a wonderful view of the Old City. A lot of young people work here: interns from Austria and Germany, some doing their year's voluntary service, and many Christian or Muslim Palestinians.

The pilgrim hostel of the Austrian Catholic church, opened in 1863, sees itself as 'an ambassador of Austrian culture in the Orient'. Its importance was made clear by the visit of Emperor Franz Joseph in 1869. Until 1918 the Austrian consul resided here. After that, ownership passed in turn to the British, Jordanians and Israelis. The hostel was not returned to the archdiocese of Vienna until 1985.

Address 37 Via Dolorosa, Jerusalem 91194, +972 2 6265800, www.austrianhospice.com | **Getting there** Tram to the Damascus Gate, then El Wad Street | **Hours** Café daily 10am–10pm | **Tip** The French Church of Veronica in the Via Dolorosa was built in the 19th century by the Greek Orthodox church, incorporating 12th-century structures such as arches from the Crusader-period Monastery of St Cosmas.

106__ The Wall of Life
The cemetery graffiti of Messianic Jews

Jerusalem is full of impressive, unusual cemeteries. And it is not only Jews who believe that the Messiah will return, here in the Holy City, and that the day of the Last Judgement will come. This means that many believers from all over the world want to be buried here. The cemetery of Messianic Christians is probably the most colourful place of burial in the city.

Behind a high wall on the main street of the chic German Colony lies the international burial ground of the Alliance Church. Originally founded in the 19th century by American Presbyterians, since 1927 it has been in the hands of these messianic Christians. The aim of the group is to reconcile Judaism and Christianity, and to combine Jewish with Christian elements in religious practice.

The visually dominant feature of the cemetery is the brightly coloured biblical murals on the long wall to the right of the entrance and on the far boundary wall at the back of the site. The American artist Patricia Solveson, who according to her own account found her way to faith after a wild period as a hippie, has depicted stories from the Bible in strong acrylic paint in six and a half years of work. They start with Adam and Eve and go on to the resurrection of Christ. With her husband Carl, she is sometimes available to lead visitors on tours of the luxuriantly green cemetery. Over 5,000 people come every year to see the Wall of Life.

In Israel, there are about 15,000 Messianic Jews. They are subject to a good deal of hostility, because some – for example the Jewish rabbinate – regard them as a Christian fundamentalist organisation that wants to convert Jews. Jesus is regarded by Jews as a renegade, and anti-Semitism in the name of Christ, with its dreadful consequences, has a history as long as that of Christianity itself. Even in the Roman Catholic church there is scepticism today about missions to convert Jews.

Address 41 Emek Refa'im Street, Jerusalem 9314101, +972 52 3806208, www.jerusalemwalloflife.org | **Getting there** Bus 34 or 49 to Emek Refa'im / HaTzfira | **Hours** Usually closed; it is best to make arrangements by telephone | **Tip** Emek Refa'im Street is a good place for strolling and window shopping. As well as cafés, restaurants, wine shops, delicatessens and boutiques, there are many buildings constructed by the German Templer group. The old Templer cemetery is accessible. Most of the names on crosses and gravestones are Swabian.

107 __ The Walled-Off Hotel

Interior and message by the graffiti star Banksy

Children would love this hotel. At the entrance are a life-size monkey dressed as a page and a porter in a distinguished-looking uniform; in the strangely lit lobby are weird objects and dolls, as well as an automatic piano. A stuffed cat clings to a bird cage at the reception desk and stares hungrily at the birds. This unusual hotel at the edge of Bethlehem, right by the border wall between Israel and the Palestinian territories, advertises itself with 'the ugliest view in the world'.

The Walled-Off Hotel (its name is a play on the luxurious Waldorf) is an all-round work of art, a political statement and a daring investment. It is a project by the graffiti artist Banksy. The nine rooms and suite are decorated with his works. A museum in the building shows dramatic photographs conveying a very one-sided account of recent history from the Palestinian point of view. On the first floor is a gallery with modern paintings, collages, sculptures and photos by Palestinian artists.

Little is known about the identity of Banksy. He is thought to be from England, and is regarded as the world's most successful graffiti artist, said to be worth more than €20 million. His financial and political involvement express a passionate commitment to the Palestinian cause, along with severe criticism of Israel. The wall makes Palestine the largest open prison on the planet, he says. The Israelis built it after 2002, when the number of suicide attacks in Israel increased dramatically. Since construction of the wall, the number of such attacks has fallen greatly.

In Bethlehem, Banksy sprayed nine template images on the security walls in 2005 and 2007 – among them a dove of peace wearing a bullet-proof vest. This graffiti work became a tourist attraction. The hotel, which was opened in 2017, is intended to promote tourism further and give publicity to the interests of the Palestinians.

Address 182 Caritas Street, Bethlehem 90907, +972 970 2 2771322 | **Getting there** Buses from the Damascus Gate to Bethlehem, then a taxi. In a hire car you cannot normally enter the Palestinian territory. The alternative is to park the car at the Bethlehem checkpoint, walk across the border and take a taxi. | **Tip** The Palestinian Heritage Centre, 200 metres away, presents items such as colourful textiles. You can buy embroidery work and other craft products (Manger Street, +972 2 2742381, Mon–Sat 10am–8pm).

108__ *Warde*

Huge artificial flowers react to passers-by

For the mainly orthodox locals on Valero Square opposite the Mahane Yehuda Market, the large, self-inflating flower-like nylon covers at the top of tall, boldly bent metal columns have long been part of the everyday scene, livening up an otherwise run-down part of the city. They hardly look up any more when, as they pass by, the bright red textile installations five metres above them open like great flowers, with street lights at the centre.

This has happened less and less often, however, since the interactive works of art were set up. In winter, the sensitive materials are taken away, and in the summer months the work, entitled *Warde*, suffers from technical problems. A few months after its inauguration by the mayor of Jerusalem at the Jewish festival of light, Hanukka, in December 2015, the fabric had to be removed from two of the four installations. They had been badly damaged by the elements.

But when *Warde* functions properly, it is a sight for sore eyes, not only for children, to watch how the four structures, which have been fitted with movement sensors, take an enlivening, entertaining part in the goings-on along Jaffa Road. The authors of the work were the creative architectural office HQ Architects, originally founded in Tel Aviv but now with a headquarter in New York. The intention was to improve, through imaginative intervention, the appearance of this somewhat run-down corner of the city, a scene of dilapidated houses, cheap shops, an electricity substation built from grey concrete and rubbish containers. The city authorities of Jerusalem acquired the remarkable objects, which provide shade during the day and additional lighting when it is dark, for several hundred thousand euros, but clearly overlooked the need for funding for their permanent maintenance. That is the reason why visitors need a little bit of luck when they want to see how *Warde* works.

Address Valero Square, Jerusalem 9762637, www.hqa.co.il/mies_portfolio/warde |
Getting there Tram to Mahane Yehuda | Tip The Art Shelter Gallery is probably the
only orthodox gallery in Jerusalem with modern art. It lies in the orthodox quarter
Mekor Baruch and only exhibits works that can be regarded as inoffensive from a
religious point of view. The gallery, housed in a bunker, is a non-profit project funded
by the city government (7 Yehuda HaMakkabi, Sun & Tue, Thu 5–8pm).

109_ Yad Hashmona

Biblical village with Finnish roots

The 'Memorial of the Eight', as Yad Hashmona is translated, is controversial in Israel, as it is run by Messianic Jews, who believe in Christ as the Messiah but practise Jewish rites and customs. However, hardly anyone who comes here will be blind to the beauty of this place in the Judaean mountains. More than 240 members of a community organised as a cooperative live here. They run a biblical theme park, a country hotel with a restaurant and conference rooms, as well as a joiner's shop, a bakery and a stables.

In 1971, a small group of Finnish Christians established the project and named it after a group of Jews from Austria who fled to Finland after the Nazi seizure of power there in 1938. The government in Helsinki deported them in 1942 into the hands of the Gestapo. Seven of them were killed in Auschwitz, and one survived. The Finnish founders of Yad Hashmona regarded their settlement, which originally lived from growing fruit, as an act of reparation and reconciliation. Since 1979, the community, whose members come from many countries today, have declared themselves to be Messianic Jews.

The centre of the estate is a large garden with equipment and buildings that are meant to give visitors a sensual immersion in biblical times. Following consultation with the state antiquities body, the biblical village was created as authentically as possible in 2000. Between terraces, trees and plants typical of ancient times, the visitor route is lined with presses for wine and olive oil, and reconstructions including a ritual Jewish bath ('mikvah'), an old synagogue and a Bedouin tent.

The community made headlines in 2008 by refusing for religious reasons to host a wedding ceremony for a lesbian couple from England. At the end of the case, Yad Hashmona had to pay compensation of approximately €20,000 on grounds of sexual discrimination.

Address Yad Hashmona, Neve Ilan 90895, +972 2 5942000, www.yadha8.co.il | **Getting there** From Jerusalem national route 1 towards Tel Aviv, exit at Neve Ilan, straight ahead to the roundabout, turn left, and after 500 metres turn right to Yad Hashmona | **Tip** The beautifully situated Domaine du Castel is a family-run boutique vineyard whose red wines are highly praised. Only locally grown grapes are used (Yad Hashmona, Haute Judee 9089500, +972 2 5358555, www.castel.co.il/en, Sun–Thu 8am–5pm).

110_ Yad La'Shiryon

Tanks of the Zionist struggle

The memorial for fallen soldiers of the armoured corps demonstrates and celebrates the military might and technical ingenuity of the Israeli forces in fighting against Arab powers. A long commemorative wall inscribed with names also preserves the memory of almost 5,000 soldiers of tank brigades who were killed.

The site was inaugurated in 1982. A number of armoured military vehicles, together with 110 tanks, built in Israel, Germany, the USA, Britain, France and the Soviet Union can be seen. Here, the Israelis display both their own tanks and ones that they captured and used themselves, most of them modified and converted. Some of the tanks are over 80 years old, and many show marks of battle. Above the site stands an M4 Sherman tank, placed more than 10 metres high on a British-built water tower. It is the logo of the museum.

The fortress-like main building that houses exhibition spaces, a library and a synagogue, was once one of 69 police stations of the British Mandate for Palestine. They are named after a police officer, Charles Tegart, who had experience of fighting against the underground resistance movement in India. He protected police stations against grenades and attacks with reinforced concrete and equipped them with slits for firing. After the withdrawal of the British in 1948, these 'Tegart forts' with their tall, fortified towers were taken over by Jewish or Arab units. In the face of many attacks, Latrun was held by Arab forces for many years, and did not fall into Israeli hands until 1967.

The Israeli artist Dani Karavan remodelled the fortified tower to make it into a 'tower of tears'. Inside it, water trickles constantly down walls of steel. In the museum rooms, the history of armoured warfare is illustrated. In addition to models of tanks, visitors also see an armoured knight, as well as Assyrian and Egyptian war chariots.

Address Latrun, Lod 71106, +972 8 9255268 | **Getting there** Buses 12, 19 or 27a to HMC (Hadassah Medical Center); national route 1 to Tel Aviv, exit to Latrun, road no. 3 (signposted) | **Hours** Sat–Thu 8.30am–4pm, Fri 8.30am–noon | **Tip** It is worth visiting the Emmaus Nikopolis site at the entrance to the Ayalon Canada Park to see the ruins of two Byzantine basilicas, a Crusader church and Jewish tombs from the time of Christ. According to St Luke's Gospel, Jesus broke bread here after his resurrection (national route 3 towards Tel Aviv).

111__ The Yvel Design Center

Socially committed jewellery workshops

The Yvel Design Center produces a large and impressive collection of original, high-class jewellery. In the south of Jerusalem its owners also present with pride a multi-faceted Israeli success story. In 1986, Orna and Isaac Levy started out with an initial capital of only $2,000 US.

To begin with, they combined organic pearls with semi-precious stones such as lapis lazuli, coral or onyx, later with diamonds, emeralds and sapphires. Yvel – the company name is simply the family name spelled backwards – became known for bold designs with pearls and precious stones set in or decorated with gold. Brooches, bracelets and necklaces won many prizes at international competitions such as the Town & Country Couture Design Award. Jewellery by Yvel is sold worldwide.

The design centre welcomes visitors on tours to watch the jewellery designers at work, and to spend time tasting wines in the cellar of a beautifully restored 19th-century pilgrims' hostel and a delightful little garden.

With their company flourishing, the Levy family also believe that they have social responsibilities. They deliberately choose immigrants for their training courses. Yvel has about 100 employees, who come from 22 different countries. As an immigrant child from Argentina, Isaac Levy himself has experience of how difficult it is to acclimatise to life in a new country. To this day, a great challenge for Israel is the integration of more than 100,000 Jews from Ethiopia. This almost forgotten Jewish minority from the north-east of Africa was brought to Israel from the 1980s onwards, sometimes in spectacular rescue operations. In 2010, the Megemeria School was set up at Yvel. It gives Ethiopian Jews a bursary for training in jewellery design and goldsmith work, as well as education in the Hebrew language, arithmetic and managing everyday life in Israel.

Address 1 Yehiel M. Steinberg Street, Ramat Motza, Jerusalem 9677149, +972 2 6735811, www.yvel.com | Getting there Bus 154, 155 or 186 to Motsa | Hours Sun–Thu 9am–5pm | Tip The Yellin House in the Motsa Valley was built in 1890 and is one of the first farms that Jews built and ran in the 19th century in the Jerusalem area. This historic building houses an information centre about the history of agricultural settlements (+972 2 5345443, www.shimur.org/Yellin).

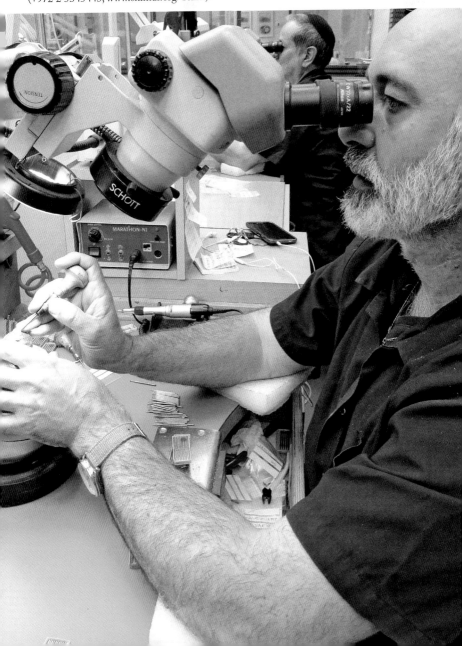

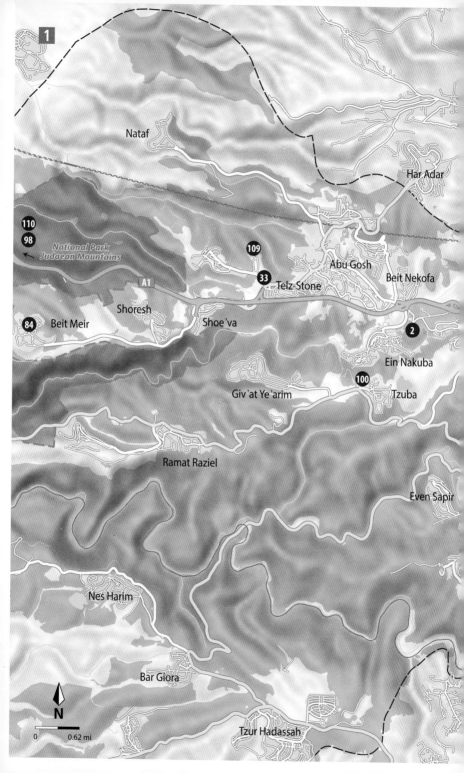

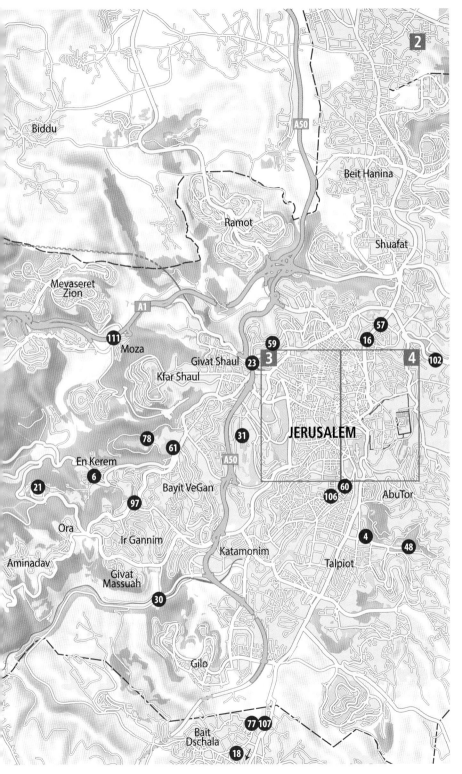

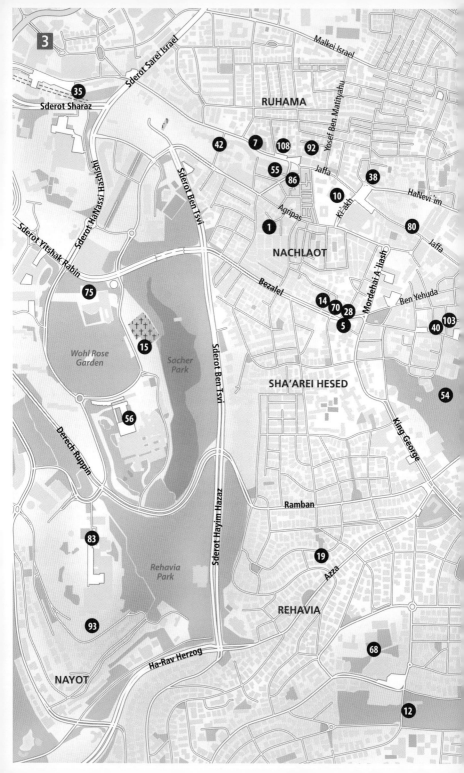

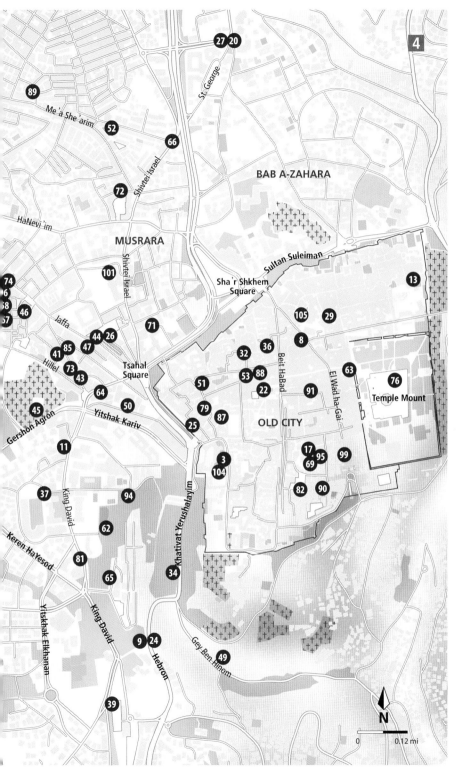

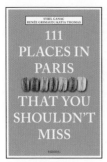

Sybil Canac, Renée Grimaud,
Katia Thomas
111 Places in Paris
That You Shouldn't Miss
ISBN 978-3-7408-0159-5

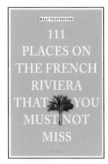

Ralf Nestmeyer
111 Places on the French Riviera
That You Must Not Miss
ISBN 978-3-95451-612-4

Solange Berchemin
111 Places in the Lake District
That You Shouldn't Miss
ISBN 978-3-7408-0378-0

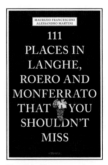

Maurizio Francesconi,
Alessandro Martini
111 Places in Langhe, Roero and
Monferrato That You Shouldn't Miss
ISBN 978-3-7408-0399-5

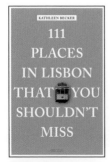

Kathleen Becker
111 Places in Lisbon
That You Shouldn't Miss
ISBN 978-3-7408-0383-4

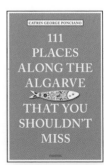

Catrin George Ponciano
111 Places along the Algarve
That You Shouldn't Miss
ISBN 978-3-7408-0381-0

Alexia Amvrazi, Diana Farr Louis,
Diane Shugart, Yannis Varouhakis
111 Places in Athens
That You Shouldn't Miss
ISBN 978-3-7408-0377-3

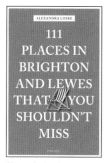

Alexandra Loske
111 Places in Brighton and Lewes
That You Shouldn't Miss
ISBN 978-3-7408-0255-4

Fabrizio Ardito
111 Places in Malta
That You Shouldn't Miss
ISBN 978-3-7408-0261-5

Tom Shields, Gillian Tait
111 Places in Glasgow
That You Shouldn't Miss
ISBN 978-3-7408-0256-1

Andrea Livnat, Angelika Baumgartner
111 Places in Tel Aviv
That You Shouldn't Miss
ISBN 978-3-7408-0263-9

Kay Walter, Rüdiger Liedtke
111 Places in Brussels
That You Shouldn't Miss
ISBN 978-3-7408-0259-2

Kai Oidtmann
111 Places in Iceland
That You Shouldn't Miss
ISBN 978-3-7408-0030-7

Thomas Fuchs
111 Places in Amsterdam
That You Shouldn't Miss
ISBN 978-3-7408-0023-9

Michael Glover, Richard Anderson
111 Places in Sheffield
That You Shouldn't Miss
ISBN 978-3-7408-0022-2

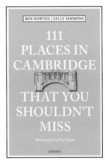

Rosalind Horton,
Sally Simmons, Guy Snape
111 Places in Cambridge
That You Shouldn't Miss
ISBN 978-3-7408-0147-2

Justin Postlethwaite
111 Places in Bath
That You Shouldn't Miss
ISBN 978-3-7408-0146-5

Matěj Černý, Marie Peřinová
111 Places in Prague
That You Shouldn't Miss
ISBN 978-3-7408-0144-1

Gillian Tait
111 Places in Edinburgh
That You Shouldn't Miss
ISBN 978-3-95451-883-8

Julian Treuherz, Peter de Figueiredo
111 Places in Liverpool
That You Shouldn't Miss
ISBN 978-3-95451-769-5

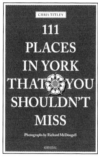

Chris Titley
111 Places in York
That You Shouldn't Miss
ISBN 978-3-95451-768-8

Frank McNally
111 Places in Dublin
That You Must Not Miss
ISBN 978-3-95451-649-0

Beate C. Kirchner
111 Places in Florence and Northern
Tuscany That You Must Not Miss
ISBN 978-3-95451-613-1

Giulia Castelli Gattinara, Mario Verin
111 Places in Milan
That You Must Not Miss
ISBN 978-3-95451-331-4

Acknowledgement

For well-informed advice and assistance in working
on this book I would like to thank Ariel Levy, Ulrich Sahm,
Dr Annemarie Fritz-Stratmann, Gisela Steinhauer,
Dr Jan Kühne and Eugen Sommer.

The author

Until 2016, **Laszlo Trankovits** was a foreign
correspondent for the Deutsche Presse Agen-
tur (dpa) for 25 years, 4 years of which he spent in Israel. He is the
author of several books, including *111 Places in Cape Town That You
Must Not Miss*. laszlo.trankovits.de